The Tragedy of King Christophe

NORTHWESTERN WORLD CLASSICS

*Northwestern World Classics brings readers
the world's greatest literature. The series features
essential new editions of well-known works,
lesser-known books that merit reconsideration,
and lost classics of fiction, drama, and poetry.
Insightful commentary and compelling new translations
help readers discover the joy of outstanding writing
from all regions of the world.*

Aimé Césaire

The Tragedy of King Christophe

A Play

Translated and with an introduction
by Paul Breslin and Rachel Ney

Northwestern University Press ✦ *Evanston, Illinois*

Northwestern University Press
www.nupress.northwestern.edu

Printed in the United States of America

10 9 8 7 6 5 4 3 2

Library of Congress Cataloging-in-Publication Data

Césaire, Aimé.
   [Tragédie du roi Christophe. English]
   The tragedy of King Christophe : a play / Aime Cesaire ;
translated and with an introduction by Paul Breslin and Rachel Ney.
     pages cm — (Northwestern world classics)
   ISBN 978-0-8101-3058-6 (cloth : alk. paper)
   1. Henri Christophe, King of Haiti, 1767–1820—Drama.
I. Breslin, Paul. II. Ney, Rachel. III. Title. IV. Series: Northwestern
world classics.
   PQ3949.C44T713 2015
   842.914—dc23

                                       2014042763

Our debts are many. To begin with those closest to home:

R.N.: I have spent endless hours discussing with my husband, Jason Ney, the points of translation for this book. I would like to thank him for his patience, passion, keen eye, and particularly his analysis of the land grading on which the Citadel was built. Without his expertise, our translation would have less clarity and accuracy.

P.B.: I would like to thank my wife, Jeanne Breslin, for her steady encouragement during my long labors on this project. Her love and companionship sustained my faith in the work.

We owe special thanks to John Saaty (Northwestern University, Weinberg College of Arts and Sciences, class of 1990) for generously contributing a subvention to defray the permission costs of this edition.

We are also grateful to A. James Arnold, not only for his encouragement of this project, but for advice and corrections in our introduction and annotations. His decision to invite P.B. to co-edit *La Tragédie du roi Christophe* with him for the Planète Libre/CNRS *Édition critique* of Césaire's works gave us access to archival materials, most notably Césaire's letter to Jahnheinz Jahn explaining unusual words and allusions in the play.

We owe a huge thank-you to the St. Lucian poet and man of the theater Kendel Hippolyte, who read through the translation with P.B. twice in June 2010 in St. Lucia, with the French text ready to hand. He suggested idiomatic Anglophone creole renderings of colloquial or creole passages and corrected our errors in creole grammar. Also thanks to the St. Lucian poets McDonald Dixon and John Robert Lee, and the Guyanese actor Marc Williams, who joined Kendel Hippolyte and P.B. for a final read-through.

Jean Jonaissant of Syracuse University reviewed our introduction and annotations, educating us about subtleties of Kreyòl usage and exchanging ideas on the translation of problematic words.

Barbara J. Newman, John Evans Professor of Latin at Northwestern University, kindly provided us with authoritative translations and biblical sources for passages in Latin.

Nick André of the Indiana University Creole Institute helped us arrive at a more accurate translation of the *vodou* songs and confirmed our translation of a problematic Kreyòl phrase at the end of Act II, scene 8.

Yves Renard of St. Lucia sent, via Kendel Hippolyte, a vivid description of Caribbean methods of readying a fighting cock for combat, which helped us in translating the prologue.

We also want to thank the staff at the British Library, the Bodleian Library at Oxford University, and the Wilberforce archive at Duke University for their attempts to locate the elusive letter (perhaps invented) from William Wilberforce to King Christophe, from which the king reads aloud in Act I, scene 7. John D. Garrigus of University of Texas, Arlington, Chris Bongie of Queen's University, Ontario, and Kate Ramsay of the University of Miami (as well as Messrs. Jonaissant and Arnold) responded to our request for help in locating this letter, though they, too, were unable to confirm its existence.

Whatever faults remain in our work are, of course, our responsibility. But they would surely have been more numerous and egregious without the marvelous help we have received.

In the introduction and annotations to this volume, we abbreviate the title of the present volume *TKC.* Additionally, we use the following abbreviations:

TRC	Césaire, Aimé. *La tragédie du Roi Christophe* (completely revised by the author). Paris: Présence Africaine, 1970.
TL	———. *Toussaint Louverture: La révolution français et le problème colonial.* Paris: Présence Africaine, 1981 [1960].
Trouillot, *SAN*	Trouillot, Michel-Rolph. *Haiti: State against Nation: The Origins and Legacy of Duvalierism.* New York: Monthly Review Press, 1990.
Trouillot, *STP*	———. *Silencing the Past: Power and the Production of History.* Boston: Beacon Press, 1995.

Anyone embarking on an edition of Césaire's work is confronted with a dilemma. Césaire was rather careless about editorial detail, and consequently, small inconsistencies and omissions abound. One must therefore decide whether to impose a consistent format or to let the inconsistencies stand. Throughout this edition, we have kept editorial intervention to a minimum. Apart from a few exceptions, which are explained in our annotations, we have stuck to translating what Césaire wrote and have resisted the temptation to correct.

At the time of his death in 2008, at the advanced age of 94, Aimé Césaire had long since become an iconic figure: cofounder, with Léopold Sédar Senghor, of the *négritude* movement; author of the long poem *Cahier d'un retour au pays natal* (*Notebook of a Return to the Native Land* [1939])—from which many Caribbean poets can quote by heart—and *Discours sur le colonialisme* (*Discourse on Colonialism* [1950; rev. 1955]), which is still widely taught in postcolonial literature courses. He had also served for decades as central Martinique's representative in the French National Assembly, as well as mayor of Martinique's capital, Fort-de-France. Despite the fierce condemnation of colonialism in his writings, the metropole claimed him upon his passing as one of its own, observing his death with full obsequies and, in April of 2011, a commemorative plaque in the Pantheon. He was famous as a poet, a political essayist, and a political leader.

In addition to his poetry and political writings, Césaire published four plays, beginning with *Et les chiens se taisaient* (*And the Dogs Were Silent*, 1956) and ending with *Une tempête* (*A Tempest*, 1969). In the English-speaking world, *A Tempest* is by far the most widely known of the four, partly because of its intertextual relationship with Shakespeare's *The Tempest*, and partly because it presents an overarching parable about colonialism, as opposed to the historical particularity of *Une saison au Congo* (*A Season in the Congo*, 1966), which deals with the rise and assassination of Patrice Lumumba, and *La tragédie du Roi Christophe* (*The Tragedy of King Christophe*, 1963; rev. ed. 1970), which deals with the period of upheaval in Haiti after the assassination of Jean-Jacques Dessalines in 1806. Although a republic continued to exist in the South, Henri Christophe declared himself King Henry I in 1811 and ruled the northern part of Haiti until October 8, 1820, when the army turned against him. Before the troops could reach the palace to depose him, he shot himself.

On Translating *Christophe*

Among those who read Césaire in the original, *The Tragedy of King Christophe* is recognized as by far his greatest play. The Martiniquan writer Raphaël Confiant, in a study highly critical of his older countryman, nonetheless singles out *Christophe*, along with *Notebook*, as the work that will commend Césaire to posterity (Confiant, *Aimé Césaire*, 157). In 1991, it became the first play by an author of color to be performed at the Comédie Française, the French national theater. On this occasion, the Comédie engaged an African director, Idrissa Ouédraogo, born in what is now Burkina Faso, though the major roles of the King, Madame Christophe, Hugonin, and Metellus were all played by white actors, and the references to vodou were cut (Pestre de Almeida 168 and note on 166). By 1991, *Christophe* had already been performed many times, with casts featuring Caribbean and African actors, in France, Austria, Germany, Italy, Canada, Senegal—and Haiti itself.

In both the Francophone Caribbean and France, this play is regarded as a masterpiece, but in England and the United States, it comes in a distant second to *A Tempest*. This marginalization, we are convinced, is not owing only to the lack of the reassuring template provided by Shakespeare's *Tempest* or its reference to an epoch of Haitian history of which most non-Caribbean audiences know little or nothing. The play's relative neglect, we believe, also owes much to its resistance to translation. It encompasses an extraordinarily wide range of stylistic registers, ranging from lines adapted from Racine and Lamartine to songs in a Martiniquan-inflected Haitian Kreyòl; from the derivative neoclassical verse of the court poet Chanlatte to the surrealist poetic soliloquies of Christophe. It also manages to take in the discourse of parliamentary debate, the language of court protocol and heraldry, the colloquial Antillean French of Haitian peasants, and the stiff formalities of military officers. In creating the character of Hugonin, Christophe's court jester, Césaire drew together elements of the fool in Shakespeare's *King Lear*, Brechtian wiseacres like Azdak in *The Caucasian Chalk Circle*, and the Haitian graveyard *lwa* Baron Samedi.

As A. James Arnold has observed, *A Tempest*, though it reinterprets one of Shakespeare's most famous plays, reduces the Shakespearian fecundity of language in favor of a severe, almost Cartesian lucidity (Arnold, "Césaire and Shakespeare," 237). Of Césaire's four plays, *The Tragedy of King Christophe* most resembles Shakespeare in its protean delight in the inexhaustible possibilities of language. In translating it, we have tried to capture in English its wide range of diction and idiom. Where the play confronts us with kinds of language in which neither of us is an expert (most notably, the songs in Kreyòl), we have consulted with experts to correct our errors. We have sought to recognize and carry into English as many as possible of Césaire's multiple meanings and connotations and to reproduce in English, as closely as possible, the subtle shifts of linguistic register in the play. We have worked to create a multistylistic English approximating Césaire's multistylistic French, which offers the surging prose-poetry of the Presenter-Commentator's paean to the Artibonite in the first intermezzo, the hyperbolic mania of Christophe's vision of the Citadel, and the incantatory death-poems that the king utters as he confronts his end. Alongside these sublimities, the play has also required us to translate bombastic political speeches (including the not-quite-correct French of the Leader of the Opposition); the rhymed, metrical verse of Chanlatte (rendered in the idiom of eighteenth-century English poetry), the nineteenth-century ballad of Ourika (in quatrains), and the satirical songs of Hugonin, many of which derive from nursery rhymes.

In contrast to *A Tempest*, which is currently available in two English translations, only one English translation of *The Tragedy of King Christophe* has been published in book form, by Ralph Manheim in 1969. It corresponds to neither of the French texts published by *Présence Africaine*—the first edition of 1963 and the revised edition of 1970—but to an acting script, of which the original appears to have been lost. It omits passages found in both published editions and includes passages found in neither (Harris, "English Translations," 33–34). In producing his plays, Césaire worked closely with the director Jean-Marie Serreau, who encouraged a good deal of improvisation and variation of the text in each new production (Laville 255). Nonetheless, the 1970 text represents Césaire's last published version, and we have accordingly used it as the basis for our work.

In addition to the textual problem with Manheim's version, it "lacks," as Femi Ojo-Ade observed, "a great deal of the spirit exhibited in the original" (Ojo-Ade 14). Manheim sometimes flattens metaphorical speech to its literal sense, missing some of the play's poetry and linguistic suggestiveness. One can get the prose sense of it (though there are errors here and there) from Manheim's translation, but much of the verbal play in the original is lost. We believe that the polysemous (and sometimes self-parodic) quality of the language in this play is crucial to its project. The language of *Christophe* explores the question: How is Haiti to de-alienate itself, discover its own voice, and enunciate its independence? And how can the play perform this quest for authenticity within French, the language of the former colonizer?

One might see the plot of the play as Christophe's attempt to realize the program of de-alienation that Césaire called *négritude* in the concrete institutions of a state, rather than in the symbolic realm of literature. Christophe, according to Césaire, "incarne la *négritude*" ("embodies *négritude*," Mbom 64), but as Régis Antoine observes, the concept of *négritude* itself is complex—"the living and dialectical unity of so many opposites" (Antoine 113)—and there has been no unanimity about its meaning. Clayton Eshleman and Annette Smith attempt a distillation of the concept on which "all interpreters of negritude were agreed": it offered values "antipodal" to those of Western "rationalism, technology, Christianity, and individualism":

> . . . not the control of nature by reason and science but a
> joyful participation in it; not the Christianity of the mis-
> sions but the celebration of very ancient pagan rites; not
> the praise of individual achievement but the fraternity
> and communal soul of the clan, the tribe, as well as the
> love of the ancestors. "A culture is born not when Man
> grasps the world, but when he is grasped . . . by it." (Esh-
> leman and Smith, 7; the quoted words are Césaire's, in
> Jacqueline Leiner, "Entretien avec A.C.," *Tropiques* I, xvii).

By this definition, Christophe's actions and language are frequently at odds with *négritude*. He speaks continually of seizing and grasping. He is obsessed with the conquest of nature by technology and rational organization: the construction of gigantic buildings, the regimentation of agriculture. He sees Haitian nature as a nullity of dust and debris, its only structures technologically primitive "Earth and thatch, crumbling mudwall" (act 1, scene 6). Nor is he any respecter of ancient primitive rites and the primacy of the community. He suppresses the African-derived religion of vodou (though it's clear by the end of the play that he himself practices it). He also transgresses against the Catholic Church, under whose auspices he was anointed king—most egregiously by having the archbishop killed (act 2, scene 7), and again when he refuses to celebrate the Feast of the Assumption in the Cathedral, saying that "If Our Lady wants to be celebrated, she will have to follow me . . ." (act 3, scene 1). And when he sets his people the task of achieving something impossible, "Against Fate, against History, against Nature" (act 1, scene 7), he rejects the organic vision of *négritude* in favor of a Faustian defiance of all natural and supernatural limits. Césaire himself, in a 1963 interview with Dominique Desanti, described Christophe as "an African Faust" (quoted in Toumson 195).

One might say that the play's insistent polysemy and clash of linguistic registers represent in large part the divided character of the king himself and the impossible dilemmas facing his country. To negate the European stereotype of blacks as savages, he constructs a court on the European model—but thereby perpetuates the alienated mimicry of Europe. To negate the European stereotype of black laziness, he sets his people to arduous forced labor—and thereby replicates in all but name the practice of slavery. To keep his country militarily strong against the threat of French invasion, he institutes an authoritarian state that his subjects experience as scarcely better than French colonial rule. As the play goes on, Christophe begins to turn, more and more, to vodou and African symbols of authority—but he cannot make of this changing allegiance a new basis for the state. The more his people turn from him and undermine his power, the more he must define himself by words rather than actions. He becomes less a king, guiding the political and economic course of his country, than a poet whose power obtains only in the realm of the symbolic.

Next to Christophe himself, the play's most dominant character is Hugonin, whose utterance is notable for its constant punning and obscene double entendres, which often ironically deflate the lofty poetry of the king. In addition to his Brechtian and Shakespearean aspects, Hugonin is also identified with the vodou *lwa*, Bawon Samdi (Baron Samedi), who, like Hugonin, delights in puns and obscenities. He explicitly identifies himself as the Baron only at the end of the play, but his obscene banter with a market woman in act 1, scene 2 seems, in retrospect, a foreshadowing of this revelation. Césaire describes him in the dramatis personae as a "mixture of parasite, fool, and political agent." Around these two central characters swirl the play's kaleidoscopic juxtapositions of farce and sublimity, vernacular and courtly French, African and European symbolism.

Our challenge, then, is to find a way of rendering in English this amazing virtuoso display: the protean French (interspersed at times with snatches of Kreyòl, Latin, and Spanish); the webs of allusion and quotation; the Brechtian inclusion of contradictory voices, the fitful illuminations that necessarily fall short of fully disclosed and fully coherent meaning. That means finding, wherever possible, English approximations of the multiple meanings of the French text, and where this is not possible, choosing the meaning that seems most characteristic of the person speaking, and most important to the context in which it occurs. It requires that we capture, to the extent that capture is possible, Césaire's agile leaping from the lofty to the ludicrous and back again.

There are also difficulties of a plainer kind. Chief among them is the rendering of the explosive word *nègre*. This word appears often—in contrast to *A Tempest*, where, apart from the description of the play as a work for "*un théâtre nègre*" and the specification that Caliban is "*un esclave nègre*," it appears only once. And it is in no one's mouth more than Christophe's. Most of the time, the word seems either neutral or honorific, as in the language of *négritude*, which transforms the racist term of abuse into a ground of positive identity. But in at least three moments, Christophe's use of this word strikes us as unmistakably freighted with pejorative connotations.

The unstable tone in Christophe's use of *nègre* arises in part from his ambivalence toward his own blackness, the conflict between his embrace of *négritude* and his simultaneous embrace of European modernity. He offers new names and titles to replace slave names; he compares himself to the Dahomeyan king Agonglo; he wishes for his people an achievement so high and astounding as to "cancel the slave ship," a glory motivated by the reversal of past degradation. But his court adopts the usages of European rather than African monarchies. He builds massive structures such as his palaces and the enormous Citadel to rival the grand buildings of Europe. He also believes the country's survival depends on rapid adoption of European standards of economic efficiency and rationalized labor. And he sees the African component of Haitian culture as an obstacle to achieving this goal.

In modern Haitian Kreyòl, the cognate *nèg* usually means a man, without racial specification. The word has lost its racial meaning in most contexts. But although contemporary Haitian speech is one context for the play, we have borne in mind at least three others, which have persuaded us to translate the substantive *nègre* as racially marked.

The first is the probable difference between Haitian speech of the present and that of the period 1806–1820, in which the action unfolds. In pre-Revolutionary Saint-Domingue, *nègre* designated a slave, while the term *gens de couleur* (people of color) was reserved for free non-whites, most of whom were of mixed race and also referred to as *mulâtres* (mulattos). Christophe grew up in that world, and his reign began only seven years after independence. The wounds of slavery were still recent and raw; Haiti, as Christophe repeatedly asserts, had to establish its autonomy amid a world of hostile, slave-holding powers. European and North American observers often evoked racist discourse to justify their refusal to establish diplomatic relations with a black king whose nation had won its freedom by violent resistance to colonial slavery. It is difficult to imagine that *nègre* had lost its racial specificity by the early nineteenth century; absent philological evidence to the contrary, we assume that it had not.

Apart from our supposition about early nineteenth-century usage, there is the context of the play itself, within which the term *nègre* usually has an unmistakably racial significance. The neutral noun *noir* was available, and in one instance (*TRC*, act 1, scene 2, 26), Césaire makes use of it, but elsewhere *noir* is used only as an adjective. In a work by the cofounder of the *négritude* movement, this preference should not surprise us. The play is partly about Christophe's own struggle to exorcise European assumptions toward which he is deeply ambivalent. He repeatedly disparages his people as lazy and frivolous—the very stereotypes of European racist discourse—and appears before us as a self-divided man, oscillating between his sense of his people as historically destined for glory and his sense that they are intrinsically worthless, awaiting a transformation that can happen only through him. At certain points, his use of *nègre* illuminates this divided sense of black identity. If we are alert readers or spectators, we recognize a difference between Christophe's understanding of the word at the moment of utterance and its meaning within the play as a whole. On these occasions—few but crucial to our understanding of the king—Césaire uses the word for dramatic irony.

Third, we bear in mind the play's transnational audience. Its first audiences were not Haitian, or even Caribbean. There was a staged reading in Belgium by Les Griots under the direction of Roger Blin in December 1963 (Toumson 194), but the first full production occurred at the Salzburg Festival in the summer of 1964, followed by a "European tour" with performances in Berlin, Vienna, Brussels, and at La Fenice in Venice, with a Paris debut at L'Odéon in 1965 (Fonkoua 350–51). In Haiti, *nègre* has been deracialized, but in Europe it retains both its racial meaning and pejorative connotations. *Le Petit Larousse* (2007) recommends the use of *noir* and cautions against the use of *nègre* because of its racist connotations. At the same time, *nègre* does not have the violent intensity of the English term of abuse, "nigger"; no English term exactly corresponds to it.

To the extent possible, we have translated *nègre* as "black." But in three instances, "nigger" strikes us as the best approximation for the abusive or ironic tone of the original. In the first, the exchange between Christophe and the chief Councilor of State (*TRC*, act 2, scene 6, 97), the king clearly intends to wound and humiliate. The Councilor has just delivered a rather timid plea for Christophe to lighten his people's labors. The king is determined to put him in his place:

CHRISTOPHE: Dites-donc, Conseil d'État, vous qui, censément, êtes la mémoire du royaume, dites-moi, qu'y avait-il avant l'arrivée du roi Christophe? Et qu'est-ce que c'était que le Conseil d'État?

CONSEIL D'ÉTAT: Sire, il n'y avait pas de Conseil d'État.

CHRISTOPHE: Non et non, il n'y avait pas de Conseil d'État, seulement quelques nègres au cou pelé. Répétez . . .

CONSEIL D'ÉTAT: . . . au cou pelé, Majesté.

This passage we have translated as follows:

CHRISTOPHE: . . . Tell me then, Councilor of State, you who are, supposedly, the memory of the realm, tell me, what was in this country before the coming of King Christophe? And what then was a Councilor of State?

COUNCILOR OF STATE: Sire, there was no Councilor of State.

CHRISTOPHE: No and no again, there was no Councilor of State, only some burnt-necked niggers. Repeat after me . . .

COUNCILOR OF STATE: . . . some burnt-necked niggers, Your Majesty.

To render Christophe's phrase as "only some burnt-necked blacks" would mute the fury of his insult. The English *n*-word captures not only his anger, but also his self-contradictory view of the people. He rejects the stereotype of the "lazy nigger." Therefore, to ask for rest is, in his eyes, to enact the stereotype and thus deserve the derogatory name.

The second instance occurs when the overseer tries to suspend work on the Citadel in the face of an oncoming storm (act 2, scene 7). Christophe seizes a trowel and says, "Je m'en vais vous montrer comme travail un nègre conséquent!" (Look, I'm going to show you how a nigger of consequence works!). This is a complex decision: the primary meaning of "consequent" is rational, orderly, or reliable. *Le Grand Robert* admits the sense "important," as in "man of consequence," though noting Littré's objection to this usage as a "barbarism." Jean Jonaissant suggested "reliable" or "trustworthy" (Jonaissant, email message). We thought that "nigger of consequence" best caught in English the ironic tone of Christophe's remark, though it departs from the primary sense. In a European context, "man of consequence" brings to mind someone like Jane Austen's Mr. Darcy, not a black Haitian with the audacity to call himself king. This ironic juxtaposition seems to us to capture Christophe's tone.

The third instance comes when Hugonin, as Baron Samedi, announces the death of Christophe. In his speech, he parodies European discourse:

Attention, all of you! While soldiers hang some tuft of foliage on their shakos; while barons and dukes switch sides for their own advantage; while amid the ruins of their dances and the debris of their orchestras, the dancing master, embodying an outraged civilization, proclaims to all the winds of history that there's nothing to be done with these niggers . . .

"Outraged civilization" does not mince words when venting its contempt for those it regards as uncivilized. To banish the word "nigger" from the play altogether would compress the wide spectrum of Christophe's moods, which range from poetic exaltation of his people to bitter abjection of them as mere mud or excrement, passively awaiting transformation by his rule. We believe that *The Tragedy of King Christophe* speaks home truths about the dilemmas of decolonization and the difficulty of shedding internalized racist conceptions of identity. It provokes rather than comforts; it offers, and demands of its audience, a complex dialectical probing of the meanings of race, power, and independence (both psychological and political). In this dialectic, all voices, even the offensive ones, have to be heard. As David Bradby remarks, the dramatic "structure is eminently Brechtian, since every judgement that appears to be made about the king and the political situation is then undermined by a different judgement in the following scene" (Bradby 148). The play may encourage us to reject racist discourse, but it does not banish it from representation.

A similarly difficult decision concerns the roll call of court titles (act 1, scene 3). The courtiers themselves find the titles ridiculous, and if one were to translate literally, an English-speaking audience would understand the joke. Manheim translated one of them, "Sale-Trou," as "stinkhole" (Manheim 23), which is surely too broad; but something like "Foulditch" would resemble certain English place names (e.g., "Shoreditch") while catching the unflattering literal sense.

The difficulty is that only some of the names have similarly comic potential, but if one translated some of them, one would then have to translate all. Moreover, these place-names are still in use in contemporary Haiti, so that a comic translation might give offense. Nonetheless, Césaire explicitly directs that all of the first act should be played "in a clownish and parodic style, in which the serious and the tragic suddenly dawn in rendings of lightning"—leaving it to his director and actors to reconcile farce and tragedy. We decided to leave the roll call in French, but to translate the names cited as ridiculous in a speech by the Second Courtier so that the audience could understand his objection:

> With our high-hat titles, Duke of Lemonade, Duke of
> Marmalade, Duke of Candy-Ditch, aren't we a sight!
> Believe me—the French will burst their sides laughing!
> (act 1, scene 3)

(As Baron Vastey points out in his reply to this speech, one could make similar jokes about French names—and, we might add, about names from anywhere else.)

Elsewhere, the French names and titles have been retained, apart from anglicizing the terms of rank ("Count" instead of "Comte," "Duke" instead of "Duc," and so on).

We also had to decide whether to translate the Latin spoken by Archbishop Brelle in the coronation ceremony (act 1, scene 4) and during his visit to the palace (act 1, scene 7) and by his successor, Juan de Dios Gonzalez (act 3, scene 2). We chose to leave these speeches untranslated. Since Latin would not have been understood by the the vast majority of the witnesses of the coronation, it should be experienced by the audience as it is by the populace, as a ceremonial rather than semantic discourse. Nonetheless, we have commissioned authoritative translations from an eminent scholar, Barbara J. Newman, which we include in our annotations. Professor Newman also has identified the biblical sources of the Latin passages. Knowing the meaning and origin of the Latin sometimes throws ironic light on the play. For instance, Archbishop Brelle recites the beginning of Psalm 126, "Nisi Dominus": "Unless the Lord build the house, those who build it have labored in vain." This text applies all too plainly to Christophe's cruelly exacting building projects and impious conduct. Christophe builds his royal house without the Lord's blessing or participation, and at the end of the play, it falls.

One might treat the Kreyòl songs in the same way as the Latin passages, leaving them untranslated and thus respecting their difference from the French. If we had done so, we would have faced a second decision: whether to leave them in Césaire's gallicized orthography or convert them to the standard Kreyòl orthography developed some years after the play was written—and if so, whether to render them in Martiniquan or Haitian form. But we decided to translate the songs, because although Kreyòl is not French, it has enough similarity to French that a Francophone audience would be able to pick up much of the meaning. To an Anglophone audience, however, the untranslated songs would be much more opaque. Some of the songs contain passages of vodou *langage*—words that have a ceremonial significance but no semantic content. We have therefore reproduced such passages as they appear in the original. We are grateful to Nick André of the Indiana University Creole Institute and Jean Jonassaint of Syracuse University for reviewing our translations of the songs and offering corrections and suggestions.

We have tried to render the songs and other passages in nonstandard Antillean French, such as the dialogue of the peasants Jupiter and Taco, in Anglophone Caribbean creole, taking especially as our model the Anglophone creole of such places as Saint Lucia or Trinidad, in which there was a strong French influence on the language. In June 2010, one of us (Breslin) went to Saint Lucia to confer with the poet, playwright, and director Kendel Hippolyte on how to achieve an idiomatic and consistent Caribbean usage. Hippolyte and Breslin read through the play together twice, making changes where the language seemed too North American. Saint Lucian poets McDonald Dixon and John Robert Lee, as well as the Guyanese writer and actor Marc Matthews, assisted with a final read-through. Our gratitude to all, and especially to Kendel Hippolyte, for this invaluable help.

We anticipate that some may be uncomfortable with our decision not to translate the Kreyòl and colloquial passages into Standard English, so as to avoid any implication that Kreyòl is "bad" French and Anglophone creole is "bad" English. The difficulty is that the difference between the vernacular and the formal, and the gradations between, would be lost—all registers would sound the same. That, we believe, would be a terrible betrayal of the play's linguistic exuberance.

If any of the Anglophone Caribbean creoles had a standardized orthography, as the French-lexicon creoles of Haiti, Martinique, Guadeloupe, and Saint Lucia do, we would gladly have used it. But those who use Anglophone creole as a written language have not pursued standardization. From the time of the first (by now classic) writings of Samuel Selvon, Louise Bennett, George Lamming, V. S. Naipaul, Kamau Brathwaite, and Derek Walcott down to the present day, the orthography of Anglophone creole has been improvised by each writer as he or she sees fit. Most writers attempt to strike a balance between accurately suggesting what each word sounds like and making the sense intelligible to outsiders. They do not seem worried that their transcription will be taken as bad English. Our versions are no more "nonstandard" than many a passage in the work of writers named above, as well as those of the next generation such as Lorna Goodison or Kendel Hippolyte. (Whether they are of the same quality is of course another question; we claim only to have done our best.)

Though Anglophone Caribbean creole does not have a standard orthography, it does have a grammar. We are grateful to Kendel Hippolyte for correcting several errors in creole sentence construction. Any that remain are, of course, our responsibility.

We have sought to provide a translation that strikes a balance between fidelity to the letter and fidelity to the spirit, mindful of both St. Paul's "The letter killeth, but the spirit giveth life" and T. S. Eliot's ironic reversal of that maxim. (Apart from adding two minor characters omitted from the dramatis personae and supplying the names of characters who appear in each scene, we have left Césaire's somewhat inconsistent formatting as it is in the original.) We hope to have conveyed something of the poetry, wit, and sheer exhilarating power of the original, aiming at a translation that would work well in the theater but is also scrupulously accurate, of use to scholars and their students.

Henri Christophe in History and Legend

As Régis Antoine observes at the outset of his monograph, *The Tragedy of King Christophe* is a history play in some respects but not others (Antoine 7). Nonetheless, Rodney E. Harris remarks that "the first thing one is obliged to note is the author's extraordinary fidelity to real persons and facts" (Harris, *L'humanisme,* 113). The events that seem too strange to be historically true—Hugonin's imitation of a dog, the king's execution of a sleeping peasant by cannon, the Gothic punishments of Franco de Médina and Corneille Brelle, the apparition of Brelle's ghost to Juan de Dios Gonzales and Christophe—are all mentioned by one or more of Christophe's biographers. Moreover, as Harris has shown, some of the most poetic moments of the play turn out to contain exact quotations from historical documents. For instance, the last line of the play (act 3, scene 9), Vastey's description of Christophe's coat-of-arms—"d'azur au Phénix de gueules coronné d'or" [on an azure field, red phoenix crowned with gold]—is taken, word for word, from the language of an edict of 1811 "announcing, in the terms of heraldry, the arms of the king" (Harris, *L'humanisme*, 119).

To the extent that both Césaire and the biographers draw on popular oral traditions concerning Christophe, they enter a liminal space between history and legend, and, as Harris goes on to remark, Césaire also freely invents—as in the long speech of Metellus, a figure mentioned by only one biographer, who devotes to him but a single sentence. Césaire also leaves things out, as in his nonmention of Christophe's son, the Prince-Royal Jacques-Henry-Victor (Harris, *L'humanisme*, 121).

Over the course of the play, the portrayal of the king becomes increasingly mythopoeic—Vastey describes him as a "force" (act 2, scene 2), and Madame Christophe eulogizes him as an "extender of boundaries" and a "forger of stars" (act 3, scene 9). Nonetheless, the Announcer-Commentator's question, "Who is Christophe?" (prologue) is worth pursuing briefly in its historical sense, because the play's myths are to a large extent myths about history, and the play thrives on a dialectical tension between the historical record and Césaire's myth-making imagination.

The line between fact (as certified by the criteria of professional historiography) and myth is never easy to draw, and harder still with a figure like Christophe, who left behind a thin documentary archive and a rich trove of orally transmitted legends. The first of his modern biographers, John W. Vandercook, in the foreword to *Black Majesty* (1928), claims: "I have added nothing to the sparse records of old books and the fading memories in the minds of men in his own country" (viii). Since the book was published 108 years after Christophe's death, "memories" must be taken to mean oral traditions received at a remove of two generations or more. Vandercook is unscholarly—he includes a bibliography but never connects a particular assertion to a particular source. He gets important dates wrong: the slave rising is said to have occurred in 1793 (32) rather than 1791, Toussaint Louverture's death on April 27 rather than April 7, 1803 (71). He invents conversations that no one could possibly have overheard and chronicled. Harris's description of his book as "somewhat romanticized" (Harris, *L'humanisme*, 114) is an understatement. But as Harris shows by analysis of parallel passages, Césaire drew extensively on this book, often coming close to its language (Harris, *L'humanisme*, 117–18).

Henri Christophe dans l'histoire d'Haïti (1931), by the Haitian lawyer Vergniaud Leconte, draws on both the oral tradition and documentary evidence, and it is much more scrupulous than *Black Majesty* in distinguishing between the two and attributing particular assertions to particular sources. Césaire's version of Corneille Brelle's death follows Leconte rather than Vandercook, and he weaves in a good deal of material from documentary sources quoted in Leconte, such as the eyewitness account of the coronation by Julien Prévost, Count of Limonade (Leconte 261–68). But despite his apparent debt to Leconte for many particulars of Christophe's story, his vision of Christophe's ruling passions and aspirations for his country is closer to Vandercook's biography, middlebrow and unscholarly though it may be. Duraciné Vaval, another early biographer of Christophe, suggests that the "legend" of Christophe passed on by oral tradition "permits profound discoveries concerning his soul" (quoted in Maurouard 81), and some of Vandercook's "discoveries" anticipate Césaire's. The play stages both the story of Christophe's career, insofar as we can reconstruct it, and the story of its meaning in the collective consciousness of Haiti—and, more broadly, of Africa and its diaspora. The fidelity to history matters because the play is in part a political critique, attempting to draw, from the tragic failure of an early postcolonial state, guidance for the decolonizing new states of the 1960s. The realm of myth matters because, whether or not it reveals Christophe's "soul," it is part of how Haitians "remember" Christophe and understand his significance within the collective story of their nation.

One measure of the play's greatness is its subtle interplay of history and myth. The mythical and the literal pull apart as Christophe, losing control of his Europeanized kingdom and finally of his own body, becomes more and more involved with vodou and African mythologies of origin. Yet Césaire understands this tension between history and myth as a fatal consequence of the king's own mythmaking project. Christophe's literalization of the mythical emerges as one of the main causes of his eventual fall.

The play begins in 1806, with Christophe's rejection of the presidency of the Haitian Republic. The Announcer-Commentator gives a brief overview of his earlier career, which is admirably concise, but some supplementary background sheds further light on his character in the play. As a "talented black," Christophe, like Toussaint Louverture but unlike Jean-Jacques Dessalines, had been spared the brutality of field labor. Nonetheless his status before the Revolution had been lower than that of his postrevolutionary rival Alexandre Pétion, the son of a white Frenchman, born free and educated in France (Fenton 375). Christophe was not born in Haiti, but probably in Grenada, on October 6, 1767. His parents were probably free, one of them probably of mixed race (Cole 30, Leconte 1). His father sent him to sea at the age of ten; the captain of his vessel "in turn . . . got rid of him to a Saint-Dominican sugar planter named Badêche" (Cole 31). At this point Christophe may have been a slave, working as a scullion in Badêche's kitchen, from which he was promoted to cook at the Inn of the Crown (L'Hôtel de la Couronne). Shortly before his twelfth birthday, he served, either "as free-born infantryman or, according to other accounts, as a slave-orderly to a French officer," in a regiment "raised from mulattos and free Negroes" by Count d'Estaing to fight against the British in the American Revolution, receiving a slight wound at the battle of Savannah (Cole 31). After this service, he returned to his job at the Cape. "Within ten years of his return to the Couronne . . . he was in effect managing the hotel" (Cole 32).

Prior to 1794, he did not take part in the Revolution; rather, his military career, which had brought him only to the rank of Captain, had been on behalf of the colonial government, not the revolutionaries. Cole surmises that Christophe probably served with the troops who crushed the rebellion led by Vincent Ogé and Jean-Baptiste Chavannes in late 1790 (Cole 32). This small-scaled, quickly suppressed rebellion, intended to secure civil rights for free persons of color, presaged the broader revolution launched by the slaves in the following year.

On August 22, 1791, slaves from a number of plantations on the Northern plain staged a coordinated rising. Many plantation owners were killed, their fields burned, and the agricultural machinery smashed. In the first three years, the Revolution settled into a standoff. The slaves were unable to defeat the colonists, but the colonists, unable to put down the revolt, had to settle for containing it within certain zones.

In June of 1793, the colonial commissioners Etienne Polverel and Léger-Félicité Sonthonax quarreled with the new governor-general of the colony, François-Thomas Galbaud, who disapproved of their support of civil rights for free persons of color. Galbaud incited French sailors from ships at anchor in the harbor of Cap Français to riot, and, during the fighting on June 20, a fire broke out that destroyed most of the town.

The chief trading port of the colony was reduced to ashes, and many white property holders fled abroad (Popkin 217–45). The commissioners had alienated the "big whites," and they faced military incursions from Great Britain and Spain, each of which hoped to form an alliance with the whites and gain sovereignty in the colony. In dire need of reinforcements, Sonthonax offered freedom to all slaves who agreed to fight for France, but in August 1793, he took the more sweeping step of liberating all slaves without conditions. On February 4, 1794, the French National Convention backed his move by abolishing slavery in all French colonies. At about the time this news reached Saint-Domingue, and probably in response to it (Dubois 179), Toussaint Louverture, who had been fighting with the Spanish against the French, switched sides.

Though he had served as "an artilleryman and as a dragoon" (Cole 32), Christophe's participation in the Revolution dates from this moment. He entered at the point where the revolutionary cause and the French cause had merged, though they would split apart again in 1802. He rose to the rank of general and was second only to Jean-Jacques Dessalines as Toussaint Louverture's most trusted military commander.

Toussaint led brilliantly, driving out the Spanish and English forces, and by the end of the decade, he had brought the Revolution to what seemed its successful conclusion. In 1801, he had been appointed governor for life and presided over the restoration of prosperity based, as before, on agricultural export, though this was accomplished by means of "a repressive labor system that Haitian historians have baptized *caporalisme agraire* (militarized agriculture) that alienated many of his followers" (Trouillot, *SAN*, 46). Without consulting the metropole, Toussaint took possession of the Spanish side of the island (the present Dominican Republic) and published a constitution. These unilateral assertions of authority angered Napoleon.

During negotiations for the Treaty of Amiens (March 1802), France reached a truce with Britain in October, 1801. Napoleon took advantage of this truce to send an army of 30,000 troops (a number later doubled by reinforcements), under the leadership of his brother-in-law, Charles-Victor-Emmanuel Leclerc, with secret orders to depose Toussaint and restore slavery. The expedition arrived in January, 1802. Christophe, pleading lack of permission from Toussaint, refused to let Leclerc land at Cap Français; to render the town useless to the French, he evacuated it and set it on fire, beginning with his own house (Leconte 62; Cole 88). But in April, in a weak military position, and perhaps crediting Leclerc's assurances that France did not intend to restore slavery (Dubois 275), Christophe, along with several other generals, submitted to Leclerc, as did Jean-Jacques Dessalines and Toussaint himself in May. But on June 7, Toussaint was lured to a meeting, taken to France under arrest, and imprisoned at the Fort de Joux in the Jura Mountains, where he died on April 7, 1803. On May 20, 1802, the French had passed a law reinstating slavery in colonies that had been captured from France and returned in the Treaty of Amiens. Once news of this law reached the colony, French intentions were unmasked, and the generals who had submitted to Leclerc resumed fighing against him. The revolutionaries, now led by Dessalines, fought with renewed tenacity and skill. Assisted by yellow fever, which killed almost half the French forces, including Leclerc himself, they defeated the invading army. After being defeated at Vertières on November 18, 1803, Leclerc's successor Rochambeau surrendered to Dessalines, who proclaimed independence, effective January 1, 1804 (Dubois 297–98). The colonial name Saint-Domingue was changed to Haïti, a transliteration of the Taino name for Hispaniola.

With Toussaint gone, Christophe emerged from the war as second only to Dessalines, who, upon assuming the presidency, appointed Christophe commander-in-chief of the Haitian army (Cole 148). Determined to root out French influence in the new nation, Dessalines had roughly ninety percent of the white population killed, a decision of which Christophe disapproved (Cole 143; for the argument that Dessalines deliberately created the "myth" of the massacre in order to scare away the French, see Jonassaint, "Textes fondateurs" 17, 1n). Dessalines continued the military style of governance established by Toussaint and enforced it more harshly. In emulation of Napoleon, he had himself crowned emperor on October 8, 1804 (Cole 145) . The received image of Dessalines, which the play does not contradict, depicts a cruel despot overly devoted to dancing and revenge. But Nicholls (38) and Trouillot (*SAN*, 46) note that he was determined to redistribute some of the land held by the *anciens libres* (i.e., persons of color already free before Sonthonax's decree of 1793) to the former slaves. It was resistance to this redistribution of wealth, as much as to his despotism, that led to his assassination in 1806. Christophe secretly supported the insurrection, which was led by *anciens libres* in the South (Trouillot, *SAN*, 47).

After Dessalines's death, Christophe was offered the presidency of the republic. He ordered the election of representatives to a constituent assembly in St. Marc, charged with drafting a new constitution (Cole 155). He sent a mulatto merchant, Juste Hugonin (in Césaire's play the most complex and fully developed character after the king himself), to observe the proceedings. Christophe's rival, Pétion, packed the constitutional convention by suddenly (and illegally) creating new districts to be represented by his supporters (Cole 155; Leconte 201). Pétion, now commanding a majority, reduced the powers of the president of the republic and augmented those of the president of the assembly—a post to be reserved for himself. "The constitution," reported Hugonin, "will be the sergeant, and you will be the corporal" (Cole 155).

At this point, Christophe refused the presidency and instead set up his own government in the North. Pétion controlled the South and most of the West, though he had to contend with some local resistance, as did Christophe. There were inconclusive battles between Christophe and Pétion from 1807 to 1813, when, "holding the whole of the North Province and almost half of the West, Christophe at last resigned himself to leaving the 'rebels' unvanquished . . ." (Cole 206).

Christophe was crowned King Henry I (choosing the English spelling of his name) on June 2, 1811. In the polemics of the Southern republic, the kingdom was portrayed as a despotism that subjected its people to virtual slavery, while the monarchy disparaged the republic as weak and indecisive. The kingdom was "frankly authoritarian and autocratic," but the republic, though in constitutional form a democracy, was in practice a "military oligarchy" (Nicholls 58–59). The republic was said to favor the mulattos, and the kingdom to favor the blacks. And yet, "[a]lthough the policies pursued by Pétion tended to benefit the *anciens libres*, while those of Christophe served also the interests of a small elite among the *nouveaux libres*"—i.e., those freed in 1793 (Nicholls 57), the conflict was not ultimately about constitutional forms, race, or class; "it was a struggle rather between two elites within a single class" (Nicholls 60). Race was not decisive: blacks were a majority everywhere, even in the South, and "most of Christophe's top ministers were mulattos: Dupuy, Vastey, de Limonade, and Chanlatte" (Nicholls 55); to this list we may add Hugonin. Christophe's "sale and granting of land benefited black and mulatto alike," whereas "the principal beneficiaries of Pétion's were the mulatto officers of the republican army" (Nicholls 54).

The received image of Christophe as oppressor of his people has ample justification in the historical record. The play does not shrink from his many acts of capricious cruelty. But Césaire's Christophe is worthy, despite his crimes, to be a tragic hero. The play calls attention to the enormous difficulties facing him as he claimed a place, on terms of equality, respect, and independence, for a nation of ex-slaves—which had recently massacred most of its white population—in a world dominated by slaveholding Western nations. When Christophe came to power, he had reason to fear that without economic prosperity and a strong military, Haiti's political independence would not survive for long.

By the time he completed the first version of the play in 1961, two years before its publication in book form (Toumson 194), Césaire had been in politics for nearly sixteen years, as mayor of Fort-de-France and a Martiniquan deputy to the National Assembly. At the end of World War II, he had supported overseas departmental status for Martinique rather than independence, believing that remaining part of France would bring greater economic security. By the 1960s, he had come to regret this decision. He had also resigned from the French Communist Party in 1956, citing its incapacity for self-criticism and its complicity in racism and colonialism (Fonkoua 252–56). He had expected great things from African decolonization, only to see many of the newly independent states turn into dictatorships or military oligarchies. The dictatorship of Guinea's Sékou Touré, whom he had admired and supported, was especially troubling. He knew firsthand how easy it was, with the best intentions, to back the wrong leader, make the wrong choice. He understood what it meant to have no choice but the lesser evil, and how hard it can be to tell the lesser from the greater.

The Tragedy of King Christophe evokes with equal power the oppression of the people under Christophe's rule and the king's struggle with seemingly insoluble problems. To create wealth, neither Christophe nor Dessalines and Toussaint before him could envision any means other than the continuation of plantation agriculture, and in this goal he was opposed by the people. "The leaders wanted export crops; the cultivators wanted land and food" (Trouillot, *SAN*, 44). Christophe succeeded in restoring prosperity: "the kingdom of the North was rich by standards of the times and, just before it crumbled, the agricultural surplus was large enough to support the development of formal education, the arts, and a growing stratum of artisans." But that was "mainly because he imposed his own feudal version of 'militarized agriculture' with an iron hand" (Trouillot, *SAN*, 48).

We cannot be sure what would have happened if Christophe had broken up the plantations, given cultivators small parcels of land, and directed agriculture toward internal consumption rather than export. But that course was more or less followed in the South and, after 1820, in the North as well. It had its own bad consequences. Boyer, who succeeded Pétion in 1818 and unified the country after Christophe's death, tried but failed to preserve the old system. During his rule, "[f]oreign visitors to Haiti observed the dilapidated state of the large plantations, and the prevalence of smallholdings on which peasants grew enough to support their families, selling the surplus at the local market" (Nicholls 68). During Christophe's reign, the French did not attempt to reoccupy Haiti, but in 1825, five years after his death, with warships anchored offshore to enforce their point, they extracted from Boyer an "indemnity" of 150 million francs for their loss of "property" (including slaves) during the Revolution. Unable to raise enough money by taxation to make the first payment on schedule, Boyer borrowed an additional 24 million francs (Nicholls 65). The indemnity was not paid off in full until 1944 and contributed greatly to Haiti's continuing poverty. We cannot know what Christophe would have done in Boyer's position, but it is hard to imagine him agreeing to such terms.

Yet the suffering Christophe inflicted on his people is impossible to condone. He submitted the peasantry to forced labor, not only on the plantations but at his seven palaces and the famous Citadel at La Ferrière, built atop a steep-sided 3,000-foot mountain. Leconte cites Beaubrun Ardouin's claim that 20,000 people died working on this edifice (Leconte 368); Ardouin was a detractor of Christophe, but Leconte, an admirer, does not dispute this estimate. The king conducted surveillance of agriculture both directly (with telescope or binoculars, or by sudden personal appearances) and through his military police force, the Royal Dahomeyans. He punished laborers for the slightest idleness (as in the cannonading of the sleeping peasant) and punished his nobles harshly whenever he suspected insubordination (as in the killing of Archbishop Brelle, Duke of l'Anse) or impropriety (as in the banishment to Thomasico of Richard, Count of the Bande du Nord). Christophe's easily roused suspicion and severe punishments doubtless provoked much of the disloyalty they were intended to prevent.

The Citadel Henry, central symbol of Christophe's vision for his people, the "patrimony" he forces them to build, may serve as illustration of the play's dialectic of historical and mythical truths. The Citadel, like the grand palace at Sans-Souci, might be considered an instance of Christophe's emulation of Europe. The king appears to share Hegel's belief that Africa is a place outside of history, and that insofar as Haiti remains African, it will remain ahistorical, inert and prostrate in mud and dust. Constructing durable and impressive monuments will signal that Haiti has entered the world of European modernity. The military benefits of the Citadel will place Haiti on more equal footing with hostile European nations. The historical imperatives confronting the king are, he believes, primarily determined by Europe. Yet the mythical register of the play, as we have suggested, embraces Africa and African-derived beliefs: the evocation of Ifé, Shango, and "the Ethiopian Memnon" in the closing valedictory lines, and above all, the belief system of vodou, shared by the people and, despite his official proscription, the king himself.

Because German engineers assisted Christophe with his building projects, some historians have assumed that the Citadel was designed and built by Germans; as late as 1967, Cole (207) refers to "the German military engineers who built the Citadel" without citing a source. But, as Trouillot points out, Leconte's biography tells a different story, naming a Haitian military engineer, Henri Barré, as its chief architect (Leconte 273; Trouillot, *STP*, 61). Vandercook (159) attributes the project to "a Haitian mulatto engineer named Henri Besse," and Besse is the name used in the play. The assumption that the chief engineer must have been European bespeaks a reluctance to imagine that a black nation recently emerged from slavery could produce such an imposing edifice.

Contradicting that Eurocentric viewpoint may have been the main point of building the Citadel. The fortress would have had some military value in resisting an invasion; it commanded much of the Northern plain from high ground. It could harbor a "garrison of 15,000" troops and withstand "a siege of several weeks" (Antoine 72). And yet it is easy, even for a scholar of literature, to imagine an invasion strategy. One would enter the country at some point far from the Citadel. After securing the countryside and establishing a reliable supply line, one would lay siege to the Citadel, just outside the range of its guns, and wait for the food to run out. The main value of the Citadel in the play—and perhaps in the historical Christophe's mind as well—is not military but symbolic. It is an icon of black achievement. In Vandercook's words, "above everything, it was to be the king's grand gesture, a dream of empire wrought in everlasting stone, a monument the blacks could turn their eyes to, lay their hands on, the essence and foundation of their pride" (Vandercook 159). Or, in the words Césaire gives to Christophe, it is "the liberty of all the people.

Built by the whole people, men and women, children and elders, built for the whole people!" It "cancels the slave ship" and sets "this people forced to its knees . . . upright" (act 1, scene 6). But as Nick Nesbitt observes, "the ambiguity of enslavement in the name of liberty is present in Christophe's very conception of the citadel" (Nesbitt 129). The king attempts to arrest the mobility of liberty in stone.

Although the Citadel may be partly understood as an attempt to out-Europe Europe, it is for Césaire, as for Trouillot and Leconte, the work of Haitian, not German, skill and imagination. Certain details of its construction—the use of "bull's blood," for instance—suggest African-derived ritual rather than European practices. Christophe imagines the Citadel as the "reposoir du soleil" ("sun's dwelling-place"). In vodou terminology, "reposoir" means "[a] tree or any other place where a [lwa] is supposed to live" (Métraux 377). In Catholic terminology, the word means "reliquary." The Citadel, then, is a haunted fortress, frequented by the deities of vodou and the primal energy of the sun; eventually, it provides a tomb, or reliquary, for Christophe himself.

Although the play does not directly engage with it, there is a similar entanglement of Western and African symbolism in the name and location of the king's favorite palace, Sans-Souci. Cole repeats a common assumption, which Trouillot (*STP*, 61) traces to an 1837 account of an American visitor, Jonathan Brown, that Christophe's palace was named and modeled after Frederick the Great's palace of the same name, in Potsdam (Cole 207). But Trouillot points out that the resemblance between the two palaces is only approximate; Christophe's is European in style but not specifically German, let alone specifically modeled on Sans-Souci Potsdam (Trouillot, *STP*, 63). While conceding that Christophe would have been aware of Frederick's Sans-Souci, he proposes another symbolic significance. Sans-Souci is also the name of a very able commander during the Revolution who fought with the revolutionaries but refused submission to the command of Dessalines in 1802. Unlike the creole leaders, Sans-Souci was born in Africa, a "Congo" skilled in an African style of guerilla fighting. After much fierce and inconclusive combat, Christophe invited him to a meeting and had him bayoneted on the spot. The palace stands very near to the place where Sans-Souci was killed. Trouillot points out that in oral tradition, Dahomey was founded when Tacoodonou defeated "Da, the ruler of Abomey." He killed Da "by cutting open his belly" and buried him beneath the palace, built "as a memorial of his victim." He named the country by combining the name Da with "homy," the word for "belly" (*STP*, 65). Christophe's palace could be understood as a ritual incorporation of a respected enemy, or, as Hénock Trouillot speculates, a countermagic to avoid the fate, prophesied by a diviner, that Christophe would die at the hands of a Congo (*STP*, 59).

Once these contexts have been pointed out, the Citadel and the nearby palace undergo a transformation into something rich and strange, rather like the structure of dreamwork according to Freud. The first-face, conscious, or "official" meaning is readily understandable in European terms: the Citadel is a military fortress on a grand scale, competing with similar structures in Europe; Sans-Souci is a palace modeled on a European style, as the protocol of Christophe's court was. But the official meaning cannot entirely repress or disavow other meanings that spring from very different beliefs, passions, and motives. The unstable relation between the conscious and unconscious meaning of Christophe's symbolic gestures drives the play: as the official meaning breaks down in the collapse of the king's authority, the repressed meanings return, as Gregson Davis remarks, "with a vengeance," culminating in Hugonin's final appearance as Baron Samedi (Davis 147). Christophe, like most tragic heroes, is a divided man.

His tragedy is, in part, his inability to reconcile the part of him that "embodies *négritude*," as Césaire claimed, with the African Faust who wants to astound the Europeans by beating them at their own game.

The Place of *The Tragedy of King Christophe* in Césaire's Oeuvre

Césaire published the first version of *Notebook of a Return to the Native Land* in 1939. It went through two published revisions before a fourth, "definitive edition" appeared in 1956—and he continued making adjustments to the poem into the 1980s. This most famous and admired of all Césaire's poems was his first book, and in many ways it set the pattern for what followed. Despite his advocacy of surrealism, with its aesthetics of spontaneous eruption from the unconscious mind, he was an inveterate reviser of his works. Not only *Notebook*, but also *Soleil Cou Coupé* (*Solar Throat Slashed*) and his first two plays, *And the Dogs Were Silent* and *Christophe*, underwent at least one major public revision. In the case of the 1948 collection *Soleil Cou Coupé*, severely cut for republication in 1961 under the title *Cadastre* (*Land Registry*), A. James Arnold, introducing his translation, with Clayton Eshleman, of the original 1948 text, argues that in the second version, Césaire, seeking a wider audience and a clearer political message, in effect "censor[ed]" the first (Arnold and Eshleman xiii). (Fortunately, we do not find a parallel problem in the 1970 version of *Christophe*, which strikes us as at least the equal of the 1963 text, with a slightly more coherent dramatic arc.)

One theme that reverberates through Césaire's work, the praise of Haiti as the place "where *négritude* stood up for the first time," is already there in the 1939 version of *Notebook* (Pestre de Almeida 15; 62–63). But it was Césaire's seven-month stay in Haiti in 1944 that took him deeply into Haitian folk culture, giving him a more vivid understanding of African cultural influence in the Antilles than he had been able to acquire in the relatively acculturated Martinique. His father had early destined him for the life of a scholar, waking him at six in the morning to study French before school. He had won a scholarship to the Lycée Schoelcher, the island's elite school in Fort-de-France. In 1931 he was off to Paris, studying first at the Lycée Louis-le-Grand, then going on, in 1935, to the famed École Normale Supérieure.

Despite the Europeanizing thrust of his formal education, Césaire also conducted an informal education in Paris, where he renewed his friendship with Léon Damas (whom he knew at the Lycée Schoelcher) and engaged in extensive conversations with other black intellectuals and poets from Francophone territories of Africa and the Caribbean, including his close friend and fellow poet-politician, Léopold Sédar Senghor, and his wife-to-be, Suzanne Roussi, whom he married in 1937. With this circle he explored questions of black identity, discovered the writings of the U.S. Harlem Renaissance poets, and cofounded a magazine, *The Black Student* (*L'Étudiant noir*). The year 1939 was a watershed one for him; caught up in his work on *Notebook*, he neglected his studies and failed the *agrégation*. With Suzanne, but without an advanced degree, he went back to Martinique just as World War II began. He took a teaching position at the Lycée Schoelcher and founded the magazine *Tropiques*.

From 1939 through 1961, Césaire published five volumes of poetry, as well as *Discourse on Colonialism* (1950; 1955). But after *Land Registry*, there were no more books of poetry until *Moi, laminaire* (*I, laminaria*) appeared in 1982. In the 1960s, Césaire concentrated on drama. The 1963 version of *Christophe* was followed by *A Season in the Congo* (1966) and *A Tempest* (1969); some critics (e.g., Toumson 225) see these plays as a "trilogy" on the resistance to colonialism. With the revision of *Christophe* in 1970, Césaire's dramatic career came to an end.

The plays of the 1960s, however, emerged from his long struggle with *Et les chiens se taisaient* (*And the Dogs Were Silent*), a dramatic poem that morphed into a play. Alex Gil remarks that "Aimé Césaire worked on *Et les chiens se taisaient* more than on any other text throughout his writing career only to have it be his most neglected" (Gil n.p.). Césaire himself referred to this work as "the nebula from which all the successive worlds of my other plays emerged" (quoted in Fonkoua 286).

And the Dogs Were Silent first appeared as a long poem in 1946, part of the collection *Les armes miraculeuses* (*Miraculous Weapons*). But Gil finds that Césaire had begun writing it in 1941; his work on this text falls into two periods, 1941–46 and 1954–57, each with its own political and social context. During the first period, Martinique was under the Vichy government of occupied France, whose representative, Admiral Georges Robert, imposed strict censorship. Césaire initially conceived *And the Dogs Were Silent* as a "historical drama based on the Haitian Revolution." This theme was politically dangerous, and Gil surmises that the first version "was written in secrecy," with hope of publication abroad. In late 1943, an early typescript had been sent to André Breton. Breton, who during his famous stopover in Martinique en route to New York in 1941 had become Césaire's friend and an enthusiastic admirer of his poetry, sent the manuscript on to Yvan Goll, the editor of *Hemispheres*. Breton had an estranging quarrel with Goll in 1944. Although he repeatedly asked for the return of the manuscript, Goll never sent it back, and so it remained in the archive of the Fonds Yvan et Claire Goll in Saint-Dié, where Gil unearthed it in 2008 (Gil n.p.)

Reading Gil's edition of the manuscript (Césaire, 1943; included in Arnold et al., *Césaire . . . Édition critique*, pp. 875–983) confirms that its hero, in published versions simply "Le

Rebelle" (The Rebel), was Toussaint Louverture; other figures of the Haitian Revolution also appear. But the historically specific episodes of this text are not well integrated with the more extensive, historically nonspecific flights of poetry; most of the time, Toussaint Louverture talks much like Le Rebelle. When the first version was published in 1946, explicit reference to Toussaint and Haiti had vanished from the text. (Césaire did go on to publish a book about Toussaint in 1960, but it was a work of historiography rather than poetry or drama.)

In 1953, Janheinz Jahn, best known for his ethnographic work on African culture and religion, wrote to Césaire requesting permission to make German translations from his poetry (Ruhe 10). In addition to his work as an Africanist, Jahn had extensive experience as an actor, playwright, and director; he had evaded conscription into the German army during World War II by serving as cofounder of a company that performed entertainments for the troops (Ruhe 11). He proposed to revise *And the Dogs* to make it viable on stage. Césaire then worked with him for three years, during which Jahn cut the work by about a third (Ruhe 17), rearranging the material he kept to form a more coherent dramatic structure, breaking up long speeches with dialogue. Césaire agreed to virtually all of Jahn's changes. Jahn's translation was published just ahead of Césaire's revised French edition of 1956. To Jahn's surprise, Césaire had backed away from most of the changes and reverted, for the most part, to the 1946 text, rendering Jahn's text not so much a translation as an alternative version (Ruhe 17). Jahn pushed ahead with his plans to put the German version on the radio and on the stage. The first stage production in September 1960 drew a divided and politicized response and was read in the context of the turbulent emergence of the Republic of Congo, whose militantly anticolonial leader, Patrice Lumumba, would be assassinated in January 1961 (Ruhe 21). Admirers considered the play a justified cry of defiance, while its politically conservative detractors saw it as a display of savage racial hatred (Ruhe, 21–22).

The Tragedy of King Christophe, finished in 1961 (Toumson 194), was published serially, one act per year, in the journal *Présence africaine* in 1961, 1962, and 1963, then issued by *Présence Africaine* as a book in 1963. Differences between the serialized text and the 1963 first edition are minor, mostly a matter of correcting errors. When Jahn read this version of *Christophe*, he proposed only a few slight changes for his German translation, which appeared in 1964 (Ruhe 22). This time, he believed, Césaire had mastered the art of writing for the theater and required no assistance.

Plans for a performance in Paris in 1963 fell through for lack of funds, so the first performance did not take place in France, but rather at the Salzburg Festival in 1964. The following year, with the help of an ad hoc group of supporters, "The Friends of Christophe"—whose membership included such luminaries as André Breton, Alejo Carpentier, Alioune Diop, Marguerite Duras, Alberto Giacometti, Michel Leiris, and Pablo Picasso—a Paris production was mounted at L'Odéon.

Christophe had drawn the interest of the director Jean-Marie Serreau, who after establishing his reputation with plays by Ionesco, Beckett, and Sartre had begun working with black Francophone playwrights. He undertook the direction of *Christophe* and collaborated closely with Césaire on *A Season in the Congo* and *A Tempest*. Serreau's death in 1973 may be one reason why Césaire wrote nothing further for the stage, though by this point his pace of literary production had slowed in other genres as well.

Serreau's productions emphasized improvisation. He believed that a play had to change in each performance, rather than being overfaithful to the letter of the script. Césaire the unceasing reviser welcomed this approach—so much so that it was Serreau rather than Césaire who remonstrated that "a play is not made of clay," to which Césaire replied that "it is not made of marble either" (Fonkoua 349). The result is that "there are, for *The Tragedy of King Christophe*, as many versions as [there have been] productions" (Laville 255).

Serreau's productions used black actors for black characters. The cast of the Salzburg performance included a Haitian choreographer, Mathile Beauvoir, and Haitian actors Jacqueline Scott as Madame Christophe and Lucien Lemoine as Vastey; the role of Christophe was taken by the Senegalese Douta Seck (Fonkoua 347).

Serreau's handling of sets and theatrical space turned constraints into stylistic virtues. He had a limited budget and often, owing to the cost of theater rental, little time to rehearse in the actual performance venue. Moreover, Césaire's play has a number of very brief scenes that segue rapidly into a new setting. The upshot was that building particular sets for each setting was both too expensive and too cumbersome, requiring as it would a halt to the action as scenery was hauled about. Serreau solved these problems somewhat differently in each production, but all of his solutions emphasized the projection of images on large rectangular screens—at first fixed, but later set up to be vertically movable. The set could be simple and inexpensive, and scene changes could be almost instantaneous, requiring only the time needed to place the players on stage, without breaking the momentum of the drama (Laville 265–66).

Just as *And the Dogs Were Silent* had been seen by its first audiences as, in part, a commentary on the emergence of the Republic of Congo and the career of Patrice Lumumba, *Christophe* reminded its early audiences of several African new states that, having begun as democracies, had rapidly devolved into military dictatorships. Moreover, Haiti itself had been ruled since 1957 by the dictator François Duvalier. Césaire, despite his fascination with Haiti, refused to visit between 1957 and

1986, when Duvalier's son and successor Jean-Claude was ousted from power (Pestre de Almeida 16). In *Christophe*, Césaire shows us an extraordinarily capable—and initially well-intentioned—ruler gradually losing touch with his people and, by the very means he employs to defend their freedom, becoming their oppressor.

Césaire's third play, *A Season in the Congo*, deals with a contemporary African crisis directly, rather than in the distant mirror of post-Revolutionary Haiti. It shares with *Christophe* a wide linguistic register, from elevated lyricism to satire (e.g., the song of the Belgian bankers, delivered in rhymed alexandrines), with a leavening of African-inflected French. Laville regards *A Season* as less successful than *Christophe*, partly because the theatrical construction of the play is less compelling, but largely because it lacks the doubling, so prominent in *Christophe*, of historical characters with mythical analogues (Laville 250–51).

In addition to the doubling of Hugonin and Baron Samedi, Christophe is explicitly linked to Shango, and his career parallels the myth of Shango, who was a mortal king before he became a god:

> Once upon a time . . . Shàngó was recklessly experimenting with a leaf that had the power to bring down lightning from the skies and inadvertently caused the roof of the palace to be set ablaze. In the blaze his wife and children were killed. Half crazed with grief and guilt, Shàngó went to a spot outside his royal capital and hanged himself. . . . He thus suffered the consequences of playing arrogantly with God's fire, and became lightning itself. (Thompson 85)

Like Shango, Christophe unintentionally destroys his own family—in his case the nation, for he presents himself as the "father" of the Haitian people. And like Shango, he dies by suicide. Hugonin, in addition to parallels with Baron Samedi and the Fool in *King Lear*, has also been likened to the African Eshu and Legba (Pestre de Almeida 183–84). *Christophe*, as we have discovered in tracing its allusions, weaves an almost Joycean web of intertextuality, creating out of its myriad strands a startlingly original design. *Season* is less polysemously dense, more explicitly didactic. But it continues to be performed—it was recently produced twice in New York by Youth Onstage! in 2009 and at Theatre Row—Lion Theatre in 2010. Gayatri Chakravorty Spivak published a new translation of it in 2011.

Césaire's last play, *A Tempest*, is, as noted above, by far his best-known among English-speaking readers. Like *Christophe*, it appeared in the journal *Présence africaine* (in 1968) before it was issued in book form by Éditions du Seuil in 1969. In this case there were significant revisions in the transition from journal publication to book (Toumson 196–97). The first performance, in 1969, was in Tunisia (which happens to be, in Shakespeare's play, the place where the court party embarks on its voyage to Naples, only to be shipwrecked by Prospero's storm).

In several interviews, Césaire discussed his intentions in writing this play. It was meant to address the situation of blacks in the United States (at one point he considered writing a piece with the title *Un été chaud* [*A Hot Summer*; Toumson 196]; this title alludes to the phrase "long, hot summer," used by the American press to describe the inner-city disturbances that erupted each summer during the mid- and late-1960s). The play presents Caliban as a figure like Malcolm X, Ariel as an analogue to Martin Luther King. It is commonly read as a simple inversion of the hierarchies of Shakespeare's play, with Caliban as the hero of triumphant resistance and Prospero as colonizer and villain, but this reading ignores the fact that Caliban does not take his chance to kill Prospero, because Prospero refuses to defend himself and that the play's final glimpse of the future portrays a stalemate: Caliban hides in the bush from an aging and weaker Prospero who nonetheless has a gun and fires randomly into the foliage, much as the steamer fires blindly on the African coast in Conrad's *Heart of Darkness* (for a commentary on this ending, see Breslin 252–57). One may infer the eventual triumph of Caliban, but the play does not stage it.

A Tempest, if read as Caliban's triumph, exemplifies what David Scott calls anticolonial romance, in which plots "have tended to be narratives of overcoming, often narratives of vindication . . . and to tell stories of salvation and redemption" (Scott 7–8). As noted above, the play's equivocal ending prevents it from entirely fitting the genre, but its thrust is in that direction. Scott regards such narratives as appropriate to the period of colonialism, when political independence was a distant goal on the horizon. But he notes that as projected futures become the present, the outcome is not necessarily as envisioned beforehand. He focuses on the attempt of C. L. R. James, in 1962, to revise his classic 1938 study of the Haitian Revolution, *The Black Jacobins*. He sees James's revisions as an attempt to recast his narrative as postcolonial tragedy rather than anticolonial romance, citing the addition of six paragraphs that ponder the question of whether Toussaint Louverture was a tragic hero. James's revisions are contemporaneous with Césaire's work on his own postcolonial tragedy about Henri Christophe, and it responds to some of the same events, especially the decline of several new African states into dictatorships. To these we must add James's disappointment in the failure of the West Indies Federation, inaugurated in 1958, which was intended to unite the Anglophone Caribbean and thus prepare it for economic and political survival after independence. By the end of 1961, Jamaica and Trinidad (James's home island) opted for separate independence (Tobago joining Trinidad as a two-island nation). Since these were the most populous and economically prosperous members of the Federation, its eventual collapse in 1966 was only a matter of time. Rob Nixon observes that Césaire's play is only one of many "appropriations" of *The Tempest* by writers from the Caribbean and Africa. He notes that "the years 1968 through 1971 saw the cresting of Caribbean and African interest in *The Tempest*" (Nixon 573), but the play's "value for African and Caribbean intellectuals faded once the plot ran out. . . . Over time, Caliban's recovery of his island has proved a qualified triumph, with the autonomy of his emergent nation far more compromised than was imagined by the generation of more optimistic nationalists" (Nixon 576–77). Nixon's explanation anticipates Scott's argument: when the future arrives, it is not necessarily the one projected by revolutionary hope, and new forms of emplotment are necessary to absorb the unexpected turn of events into a compelling narrative. And yet, as Césaire maintained in an interview, *Christophe*, though tragic, is not a counsel of despair: "The triumph of Christophe is not in the present: there is obviously a defeat, but in reality Christophe has worked for the future and has nonetheless laid the foundations of a world" (Attoun 102). As Madame Christophe says in the final scene, Christophe was, despite his tragic failure, an "extender of boundaries."

A Tempest will continue to command attention as a classic instance of the anticolonial appropriation of Shakespeare's play. (Since Nixon's article appeared, there have been postcolonial feminist *Tempests*, turning attention to Miranda and Sycorax instead of the conflict between Prospero and Caliban [see Zabus, 2002].) But *Christophe* sees more deeply than *A Tempest* into the problems that do not disappear with the acquisition of nominal sovereignty; its account of Christophe's struggles to protect his kingdom from military coercion and economic exploitation speaks to the situation of postcolonial societies now as well as in the 1810s.

Ralph Manheim's translations of *Season* and *Christophe* were, for decades, the only ones available. At present there are two available versions of *A Tempest* and *Season*, but only one, with the textual and stylistic problems noted above, of *Christophe*. We have done our best, in our new translation, to let the greatness of the play shine through in English, conveying at least some sense of Césaire's astonishing achievement.

The Tragedy of King Christophe

DRAMATIS PERSONAE

In order of appearance:
PÉTION, *president of the republic*
CHRISTOPHE, *former slave, former cook, former general, king of Haiti*
HUGONIN, *a mixture of parasite, fool, and political agent*
VASTEY, *baron, Christophe's secretary*
THE MASTER OF CEREMONIES
MAGNY, *Duke of Plaisance, general*
CORNEILLE BRELLE, *Duke of l'Anse, first Archbishop of the Cape*
THE PRESIDENT OF THE COUNCIL OF STATE
THE KING OF ARMS
METELLUS, *chief of the rebels*
THE LEADER OF THE OPPOSITION
DEPUTIES
CHANLATTE, *official poet*
PRÉZEAU, *confidant and factotum of Christophe*
MADAME CHRISTOPHE, *former servant at an inn, the queen*
MARTIAL BESSE, *engineer*
APPRENTICE RAFT-KEEPER
RAFT-KEEPER CAPTAIN
THE ROYAL DAHOMEYAN
GUERRIER, *Duke of l'Avancé, general*
ISABELLE
RICHARD, *Count of the Bande du Nord*
FRANCO DE MÉDINA, *agent of the king of France, Louis XVIII*
THE COUNCIL OF STATE
TROU BONBON, *count*
JUAN DE DIOS GONZALES, *curate, afterward Archbishop of the Cape
following the death of Corneille Brelle*
STEWARD, *Englishman, doctor to the king*
AFRICAN PAGE
BOYER, *general of the army of Pétion*

Announcer-Commentator, courtiers, choir, citizens, peasant men and women, laborers, soldiers and officers, porters, courtesans, ladies of the court, echoes, distant drummers.

PROLOGUE

[*A circle of stakes defines an arena. It's a cockfighting pit, where the favorite Haitian pastime is performed. A crowd of black people. Blue peasants' clothing. An impassioned and heated atmosphere.*]

A PASSIONATE VOICE: Go, Christophe, go!

A SECOND, NO LESS PASSIONATE VOICE: Don' ease up, Pétion! Don' ease up, Pétion!

THIRD VOICE: It just ent natural! You tell me he ent greased with snake oil or chicken-hawk fat!

PASSIONATE VOICE: Hit him, Christophe! Strike!

A PLEADING VOICE: Come back on him, Pétion!

[*Fury of claws and flying feathers in an anguished silence. The birds fight ferociously.*]

A ROARING VOICE [*breaking the silence*]: Take him out! Take him out! Take him out!

A VERY CALM VOICE: Game-Master, pick up Pétion.

[*The Cariador, master and manager of the games, strokes the rooster.*]

THE VOICE: Out ent dead!

SUPPORTERS' VOICES: Give him some cane juice to pick him up.

SECOND VOICE: Blow air on him! Air, that's what he needs!

JEERING VOICE: Cluck! Cluck! Cluck! . . . Pétion's a yard-fowl!

DEFIANT VOICE: No, sir, a cock of the finest beak! Rub his legs with some ginger.

THE CROWD: Set him up! Let's go!

[*The combat furiously resumes.*]

VOICE OF THE CROWD: Go, Pétion, go! Christophe! Christophe!

VOICE: Fantastic! He's stronger than Great Drummer, stronger than Peck-Out-His-Eye!
     O Mother, what a jook in the eyeball!

[*One of the cocks falls down stone-dead. The ecstasy reaches its climax.*]

THE CROWD: Yay! Yay! Yay!

ANNOUNCER-COMMENTATOR: After this feathery battle, let's catch our breath and speak of things plainly. Yes, that's been the custom of this country lately. In the old days, you'd name the cocks "Tambour-Maître" or "Becqueté-Zié," or, if you like, Great Drummer and Peck-Out-His-Eye. Now, we name them after our politicians. Here's Christophe, there's Pétion. I didn't like it at first. But when you think about it, by God! As a fashion it's no sillier than the rest. A king . . . a president of the republic, they're sure to be at each other's throats! And if so, their names are good names for fighting-cocks. But, you'll say, things are simple for fighting-cocks, more complicated for men. Not really.

You just have to understand the situation and know the characters the cocks are named for. Who is Christophe? Who is Pétion? My role here is to tell you.

In the island of Haiti, formerly a French colony called Saint-Domingue, there was at the turn of the nineteenth century a black general. His name was Christophe. Henri Christophe, Henri with an *i*.

Oh, he didn't start out as a general. He'd been a slave, more precisely a slave-chef. He was among those called, in Saint-Domingue, "talented blacks," which meant a black with some sort of special skill. He was the chef, I tell you, at the Inn of the Crown. (Remember this sign, it bears the stamp of objective chance.) At the Inn of the Crown, in the town of Cap-Haïtien, known then as Le Cap-Français.

And it was precisely against the French that he played a leading role in the struggle to liberate his country, under the command of Toussaint Louverture. Once independence was won and Haiti arose from the smoking ashes of Saint-Domingue, and a black republic was founded on the ruins of the most beautiful of all the white colonies, Christophe quite naturally became one of the dignitaries of the new state. There he was, General Christophe in all his glory, the most feared and respected commander of the Northern Province, a Father of the Country, as they call men of that type in the Caribbean. And so, with the death of the first head of state Dessalines, the "Founder," all eyes turned spontaneously to Christophe as successor. He was named president of the republic. But as I told you, he'd been a chef, which is to say a skilled politician. And as a chef, he judged the dish a bit lacking in spices, the position given him far too skimpy a serving of meat.

So, leaving the town of Port-au-Prince to the mulattos and their commander, Pétion, he set up his rule in the Northern Province. To make a long story short, there were two neighboring states, not very neighborly, within Haiti: the republic in the South, with Pétion as president, and in the North, a monarchy.

There you see it: Christophe, Pétion, two master fighting-cocks, two "Maîtres-Caloge," as we say in the islands.

Yes, Christophe was a king.

A king like Louis XIII, Louis XIV, Louis XV, and some others. And like all kings, all true kings, I mean all *white* kings, he created a court and surrounded himself with a nobility.

But let's not reveal too much.

Give him honor to whom honor is due! Behold Henry I, Henry with a *y*. That's enough out of me. I give you Haiti!

[*In the distance, cries of the cockpit. It is the voice of Haiti.*]

Go, Christophe, go!

[*The curtain rises on* The Tragedy of King Christophe.]

ACT I

[*The entire first act is in a clownish and parodic style, in which the serious and the tragic suddenly dawn in rendings of lightning.*]

SCENE 1

PÉTION: In recognition of your service as former companion-in-arms of Toussaint Louverture, in recognition of your service as senior general of the army, we the Senate confer upon you, by unanimous vote, the presidency of the republic.

CHRISTOPHE: The law is clear. The position indeed is mine by right. But what the fundamental law of the republic gives me, a law passed under conditions of dubious legality takes back from me.

The Senate names me president of the republic, because it would be dangerous to rub me the wrong way, but it has emptied the office of its substance and my authority of its marrow. Yes, yes, my masters, I know that, under your Constitution, Christophe would be only a cheerful fellow carved in ebony, a jolly jacquemart, busily striking the hours of your law on the clock of his impotence with a ridiculous sword, for the crowd's amusement.

PÉTION: You are unjust to the Senate.

If you look at fresh milk too closely, you're bound to see some black hairs. The position we offer you retains its prestige and importance. It is the highest in the republic. As for the adjustments to the Constitution that the Senate believed necessary, I do not deny that they diminish the powers of the president, but it cannot escape your notice that for a people who suffered under Dessalines, the most frightening danger bears but one name: tyranny. And in truth, the Senate would have been unpardonably negligent had it not taken such necessary measures to protect against this menace always suspended above our heads!

CHRISTOPHE: I'm not a mulatto who parses words. I am a soldier, an old master of arms, and I'll say this plainly: the Senate's changes to the Constitution are an act of defiance against me, against my person; these are measures to which my dignity will never submit.

By thunder! A power with neither crust nor crumb, a thin slice, a plate-scraping of power, that's what you offer me, Pétion, in the name of the republic.

PÉTION: I regret that I have not made myself clear. I speak of principles, but you persist in speaking of yourself. But we have to settle this matter. Is that the response you wish me to report to the Senate?

CHRISTOPHE: Wouldn't Pétion be delighted to take me at my word?

PÉTION: And why do you say that?

CHRISTOPHE: Because Pétion is clever, terribly clever, and so it cannot escape him that if Christophe refuses power, it will be offered to him.

PÉTION: The Devil! Why would I accept what you disdain? Why should that which your sensitive teeth reject as bitter fruit taste in my mouth like a sweet apple?

CHRISTOPHE: Because Pétion is clever. Terribly clever! As soon as the mulatto Pétion has accepted the empty power that you have just offered me, the miracle will occur. Our good friends in the Senate, the mulattos of Port-au-Prince, will admirably play the compassionate—not to mention lucrative—fairies and refill his basket. Take it, Pétion, take it! You'll see, it's a magic beggar's-bowl!

PÉTION: So that . . .

CHRISTOPHE: So that the modification of the Constitution is nothing but a crass scheme to separate me from power, in the guise of conferring it on me!

PÉTION: And you let yourself be separated!

CHRISTOPHE: Fire and damnation! Let myself be separated? Oh no, Pétion! If you teach a monkey how to throw stones, some day the student might pick one up and break your head with it. Tell that to the Senate from me. They'll understand.

PÉTION: The Senate will understand that you can no longer be considered anything but a rebel general.

CHRISTOPHE: And that is of no importance. If you want an official response, a noble response, the kind your Solons and Lycurguses of Port-au-Prince love, tell them that I regret that under these circumstances—and because of the spirit of resentment against me—they have not understood that for now, in the midst of our misfortunes, the greatest need of this country, of this people who must be protected, must be corrected, must be educated, is . . .

PÉTION: Liberty.

CHRISTOPHE: Liberty, no doubt, but not an easy liberty! And that is why we have a State. Yes, Mr. Philosopher, something thanks to which this people of transplants roots itself, buds and blossoms, throwing in the face of the world its perfumes, the fruits of its flowering; why not say it, something that, if need be by force, obliges it to be born to itself and to surpass itself. That is the message, a bit too long no doubt, that I charge my officious friend to deliver to our noble friends of Port-au-Prince.

[*In a terrifying tone, contrasting with the previous relaxation*] As for the rest [*he draws and brandishes his sword*], my sword and my right!

SCENE 2

[*The Cape. Public square—view of the bay. Boats on the horizon. Stirring of black women spreading out vegetables, fowl, sugar, and salt on the ground. Cauldrons covered with banana leaves, cooking in the open air. Groups of citizens among whom circulate the agents of Christophe, Hugonin being one of them.*]

MARKET WOMAN: Sugar candy! Sugar candy! This way—I got all a man can desire! *Tafia! Clairin!* Tobacco twists! Long tobacco! Aiguillettes! Slices of meat!
   [*To Hugonin*] Some sugar candy, Papa, or a slice of meat?

HUGONIN: Hey, gorgeous, it ent that sugar I want, it's yours! And it ent that meat I go slice! I coming after you like a army, sweet thing!

MARKET WOMAN: Rude little devil! Sirs, this way for corn mash. Corn mash! Corn mash!

HUGONIN: Forget about corn mash—I'll do my mashing with you!

MARKET WOMAN: Worthless scoundrel! Help! Help! Police!

FIRST CITIZEN: But isn't it strange how that ship that keeps showing up for the last two months at the mouth of the port never gets permission to enter?

HUGONIN: Booboo! Don't you know what that is?

[*Singing*]

> *That is the whale that tacks and veers,*
> *Steering his pretty vessel—*
> *Let him bite one finger of yours*
> *And he'll eat you down to the gristle!*

Rough translation: That's the ship of the King of France. I'll tell you about its fine cargo, in case you require it: if Monsieur has need of bludgeons to cure lumbago, the hold is full of them.

FIRST CITIZEN: Sir!

HUGONIN: And if the back parts of Monsieur wish to be carbonadoed, same-same! In the hold of that ship there is everything to satisfy the wishes of Monsieur's backside.

FIRST CITIZEN: Don't be melodramatic, sir. For all we know, these people have come to propose a settlement. My God, to spare this country another upheaval, why not?

HUGONIN: Well, look at that! Monsieur has a delicate heart, he wants to avoid upheavals! My poor friend, settlements will accomplish nothing. Nor your prudence. Nor your cowardice. Like women seized with the falling sickness, never mind where or when, there are countries of upheaval, countries of convulsion, and ours has been chosen as one. That is its fate, understand? No, you don't understand. Never mind!

[*Notable persons arrive, among them Vastey.*]

VASTEY: Go, citizens! Return to your homes. That ship is not your concern. It is Christophe's. To each his own work. Yours is labor, free labor since you are free men, labor for a nation in peril. It is for Christophe to protect us, our goods, and our freedom.

SECOND CITIZEN: Well said! Christophe, that's a man, he got balls. Not like that limp-dick Pétion! They say that to get the French king to recognize him, he's offered to pay reparations to the former colonists! A Black man offers to pay reparations to those whom Blacks so rashly deprived of the privilege of owning Blacks!

[*He laughs bitterly.*]

HUGONIN: What are you whining about? You know the song:

> *I'll sell you my cow,*
> *Good for butter,*
> *Good for milk,*
> *Good for calving.*
> *A plate of cod*
> *And the deal is sealed—*
> *My cow has been sold.*

Christophe is a man, yes. Yet some things in our situation are—though not as much as Pétion's—his fault, just a bit.

SECOND CITIZEN: Be careful what you say, sir. Certain comparisons are offensive. Offensive and dangerous!

VASTEY [*indulgently*]: It's to you, citizen, that *I* say be careful. You must admit it: the French—and this still creates a dangerous situation—hold us in scant esteem.

FIRST CITIZEN: Of course, since we're black!

VASTEY: Yes and no. Grasp what I'm saying. What do the whites of France say? That Pétion and Christophe are two weaklings. The French, don't you see, have no respect for republics. Napoleon has shown us that clearly. And what is Haiti? Not one, but two! Two republics, sir.

FIRST CITIZEN: That's true. But what shall we do, my God, what?

VASTEY [*raising his voice as if haranguing the crowd*]: The whole world is watching us, citizens, and its multitudes think that black men lack dignity. A king, a court, a kingdom—*that*, if we want respect, is what we must show them. A leader at the head of our nation! A crown on that leader's head. That, believe me, would calm those heads in which windy ideas could, at any moment, unleash a storm on our own heads right here!

[*At this moment, Christophe appears on horseback, amid his glittering officers.*]

THE CROWD: Long live Christophe! Long live the man Christophe!

HUGONIN: Long live the *king* Christophe!

CHRISTOPHE: Enough! What is this people, which has, for a national consciousness, only a pudding-stone of assorted gossip? Haitian people: Haiti has less to fear from the French than from herself! The enemy of this people is its indolence, its shamelessness, its hatred of discipline, its spirit of sensual torpor. Sirs, for the honor and survival of this country, I won't have it said in the world, or whispered even, that ten years of black freedom, ten years of black negligence and irresponsibility, will suffice to squander the treasure that our martyred people amassed in a hundred years of labor and blows of the whip. Which is to say that with me, from now on, you have no right to get tired! Go, sirs! Go, disperse yourselves!

THE CROWD: Long live Christophe!

HUGONIN: Long live the man Christophe!

THE CROWD: Long live the king Christophe!

SCENE 3

[*At the palace.*]

THE MASTER OF CEREMONIES: All right then, sirs, all right. Excuse me for rushing you, but the king might show up anytime now, so we have to begin our rehearsal. I will take attendance and remind you of the general principles of the ceremony. An important ceremony. A momentous ceremony, sirs, toward which the whole world will turn its eyes.

[*Apelike, ironic contortions of the courtiers.*]

FIRST COURTIER: His Grace the Duke!

SECOND COURTIER: His Excellency the Count!

THIRD COURTIER: Oh, my prince!

[*Peals of laughter.*]

FIRST COURTIER: What a story! This king, this kingdom, this coronation, I just can't believe it is happening.

SECOND COURTIER: You may not believe it, but you sure can feel it! It's exhausting!

VASTEY: For a black king, a purple pageant, right? This black kingdom, this court, a perfect replica in black of the best old Europe has to offer!

MAGNY: My dear Vastey, I'm an old soldier. I served under Toussaint and Dessalines and I'll tell you frankly that I'm ill-suited to these court-style manners that you seem to find so delightful.

VASTEY [*very dignified*]: My dear colleague! Magny! You! The Duke of Plaisance! Restrain your tongue!

SECOND COURTIER: With our high-hat titles, Duke of Lemonade, Duke of Marmalade, Duke of Candy-Ditch, aren't we a sight! Believe me—the French will burst their sides laughing!

VASTEY [*ironically*]: Man of little faith! Come now! The laughter of Frenchmen can't embarrass me. Marmalade, why not? Why not Lemonade? These are names that will fill your mouth! A *gastronomique* for your every wish! After all, the French have their Duke of Foix (foie gras, anyone?) and their Duke of Bouillon. Are those more enticing? There are precedents, you see. As for you, Magny, let's speak seriously. Have you not noticed whom Europe has sent us, upon our request for help from the International Technical Guidance? Not an engineer. Not a soldier. Not a professor. A master of ceremonies! Form—that, dear sir, is civilization! The proper forming of men! Think of it, think! Form, the womb from which arise being, substance, the Man himself. Everything, really. The void, yet a prodigious void, generator and shaper . . .

MAGNY: What does this nonsense mean?

VASTEY: There is one who instinctively understands it: that is, Christophe. With his magnificent potter's hands, kneading the clay of Haiti, he at least . . . I won't say he knows, but better still, he senses—smelling it, the serpentine path of the future—the form itself. That is something, believe me, in such a country as ours!

MAGNY: Go stuff your precious esthete's musings! If he'd trusted in me, instead of getting himself anointed with a dab of cocoa butter and wreathing his head with a crown, he'd have strapped on his baldric, and with swords in our fists, we'd have spurred our horses toward Port-au-Prince, where there are many good lands up for grabs and scoundrels to cleave in pieces!

HUGONIN: I am no fighter . . . no, I don't follow the sword. And I'm no minister covered with lace. And yet, one has one's own little idea on the matter. It was inspired, do you understand, inspired, this idea to invent a nobility. For the king, it's a way to baptize whomever he wants, and a way to become every Haitian's godfather. Of course, if the husbands let him, he'd be everyone's *father* instead! And if I'd been a minister, there's a proposition I'd have introduced to his Council and made to the king.

MAGNY: Here's what we've come to, Vastey. A court, some nobles . . . and the King's Jester!

HUGONIN: For some while now, it's been raining titles all over. By God, that one's as good as the next. I accept it and welcome it. Now then, to try on my role for the first time,

I propose that the child the king has made with the certain plump lady you know of should be called the Duke of Varieties!

VASTEY: The riddle may well be our national trademark, but I assure you this one eludes my understanding.

HUGONIN: Ah, you see—you don't know everything!

[*Big laugh from the courtiers.*]

But look out, here he is! Damn it, the small of my back is itching.

[*The courtiers rectify their posture.*]

THE MASTER OF CEREMONIES [*seeing Christophe*]: Sirs, I entreat you, let's have some silence. I shall call the roll:
His Magnificent Grace the Duke of Limonade
His Magnificent Grace the Duke of Plaisance
His Serene Highness the Marquis of Avalasse
His Magnificent Grace the Duke of Dondon
His Magnificent Grace the Duke of Marmelade
His Excellency the Count of Trou-Bonbon
His Excellency the Count of Sale-Trou
His Excellency the Count of Bande du Nord
Squires:
    Jean-Louis Lamour
    Tonton Cimetière
    Jean-Jacques Sévère
    Étienne Registre
    Solide Cupidon
    Joseph Almanzor
Officers of the Royal Dahomeyans:
    Mr. de Jupiter

Mr. Pierre Pompée

Mr. Lolo Jolicoeur.

Good! Everyone's here. Mister Paraviré, and you, keepers of the king's store, be careful with the royal ornaments. As for their traditional use, I remind you to proceed in the following order: ring, sword, mantle, hand of justice, scepter. Let's get on with it.

CHRISTOPHE: Good, good! Very well! But we're terribly short of women! Let those ladies come in and assign to each of them her rightful place in the ceremony.

[*The ladies enter: big-bottomed, gaudily dressed black women. Christophe pats several rumps.*]

Very well, Madames Marquises, Madames Duchesses, my dear Chevaliers.

[*The Ladies take their places.*]

. . . Madame Syringe, Madame Little-Hole, Madame Knocks-Out-Your-Eye. My dear gossip!

[*The courtiers hurry to disentangle themselves as best they can in a sort of ridiculous and maladroit rehearsal.*]

THE MASTER OF CEREMONIES: Your bearing! Attend to your bearing! No angular, jerky gestures . . . rounded gestures. Neither the stiff air of a soldier on maneuvers nor a careless nonchalance of African feet and creole arms. An air at once dignified and natural . . . natural and solemn.

CHRISTOPHE [*explosively*]: For God's sake! Who sent me these bozos! Sale-Trou, come on! You're just walking any old how—it's as bad as insulting me! [*Seizing Trou-Bonbon by the collar*] . . . And no, you will not present the scepter like that! I'm not going to eat you. You'd think he was offering an elephant a banana!

THE MASTER OF CEREMONIES: Gentlemen, begin again! Attend to your bearing! All is revealed in your bearing!

[*Pompous and technical*] Here, to walk well, you must hold yourselves straight without stiffness, direct your legs in a line, never move to the left or the right of your axis, make your body participate imperceptibly in the collective motion.

[*The courtiers apply themselves.*]

CHRISTOPHE [*relaxed, then gradually growing more animated*]: It's a lofty thought, gentlemen, and it pleases me to see that you've fully grasped it! In all its profound seriousness!

These names, these noble titles, this coronation!

Long ago, someone stole our names!

Our pride!

Our nobility, someone—oh, yes, *someone*—stole them from us!

Pierre, Paul, Jacques, Toussaint! Someone branded us with these marks of humiliation, *someone* destroyed our true names.

Even mine.

I, your king.

Do you feel the grief of a man who does not know what his name is? Or what his name means? Alas, none but Mother Africa knows. Well, claimed or unclaimed, we have to decide. And I say, "claimed." It's ourselves that we claim in our names! We, who were torn apart, must do the tearing. Ourselves, our names—since we cannot tear them free of our past, we'll have to tear them free in our future.

[*Tenderly*] Now
I will cover your slave-names with names of glory,
Our names of disgrace with proud names,
Our orphaned names with names of redemption!
It's of a new birth, gentlemen, that we speak!
[*Contemplating the royal ornaments*] Mere baby's rattles,
no doubt,
But rattles are shaken!
Stony islet, thousands of half-naked blacks
The sea vomited up one evening
From whence they came, with their odor of hunted
beasts,
A shaking, an earthquake, a white savannah
As my old Bambara ancestors said,
A shaking with power to speak,
To do, to construct, to build,
To be, to name, to bind, to remake—
Well, then, I will take it all,
I well understand its weight
And will carry it.

[*The lights fade out. When they return, the setting is now the Cathedral at Le Cap.*]

SCENE 4

CORNEILLE BRELLE [*officiating*]: *Profiterisne charissime in Christo Fili et promittis coram Deo et angelis deinceps legem justiciam et pacem, Ecclesiae Dei popoluque tibi subjecto facere ac servare . . . ac invigilare ut pontificibus Ecclesiae Dei condignus et canonicus honos exhibeatur?*

CHRISTOPHE: *Profiteor.*

[*The deacon presents the Gospels, and Christophe kisses them. The archbishop places the crown on his head.*]

THE PRESIDENT OF THE COUNCIL OF STATE: Excellency, by the grace of God and the constitutional law of the nation, we proclaim you Henry I, sovereign of the islands of Tortuga, Gonâve, and other adjacent isles. Destroyer of tyranny, regenerator and benefactor of the Nation of Haiti, first crowned monarch of the New World.

[*Cries from the audience: "Henry, may he live forever! Henry, may he live forever!"*]

CHRISTOPHE [*standing, his arms open in front of the Gospels*]: I swear to maintain the integrity of our territory and the independence of the kingdom: I will never permit on any pretext whatsoever the return of slavery or any measure contrary to the freedom and full exercise of civil and political rights by the people of Haiti, and I will govern with only one end in view: the interests, happiness, and glory of the great Haitian family of which I am the head.

KING OF ARMS: The great and august Henry, King of Haiti, has been crowned and enthroned.
Henry, may he live forever!

CROWD: Henry, may he live forever!

CHORUS [*singing*]:
Henry, valiant warrior
Open for us victory's door,
Henry, valiant warrior!

[*The song transforms itself into a hymn and dance to Shango.*]

Shango, Madia Elloué [*repeated*]
Azango, Shango Madia Elloué [*repeated*]
Sava Loué
Sava Loué
Azango, Shango Madia Elloué

CHRISTOPHE [*alone*]:
Aha!
Sprung from the lowest stooping,
The depths of suffering,
The sun suddenly standing upright
Over the heads
Of a people accursed,
I set you down, gold
Rod of command!
Rod of command,
Around you, I,
Of my once-servile race,
clench my fist!
I clench! Our fists!

SCENE 5

[*A battlefield during the Haitian civil war. Night is falling.*]

MAGNY: Didn't I tell you to kill all the wounded?

THE OFFICER: This one, General, is the chief of the rebels, and
I thought you should decide what to do with him.

MAGNY: Very well. Are you, Metellus, the chief of the rebels?

METELLUS: I am indeed.

MAGNY: Why this resistance? What have you got against Christophe? Speak!

METELLUS:

    Lashed by the hard whip of a dream,
    I stumbled from stone to stone,
    down to your threshold, O Death, descending
    as I called to you
    Bédoret, Ravine-à-Couleuvres, Crête-à-Pierrot,
    Plaisance,
    places unpleasant to be in,
    all this I have borne:
    pierced to the bone by the rains,
    by the briars, by fevers and fear,
    to be hungry,
    to sleep with eyes open in morning dew
    and the dew of the night, to flee,
    having fought, having feared when we seized fate
    by the collar, beside
    Toussaint!
    That was the glorious blood of combat!
    Everywhere, along wild paths, on steep narrow passes,
    amid the barking of rifles,
    we would see the daughter, Hope
    (the palms of her hands shone in the night
    of her skin, like the gold in the dark hollows
    of star-apple leaves).
    We would see her,
    we (with our pus dried by the red leaf-coral),
    dancing
       with bare, undaunted breasts
       and unbroken blood
    (she was the mad woman who fearlessly called
    to our timid blood,
    not letting it tempt us to settled pastures and easy sustenance).
    That was a glorious, raucous blood,
    and bitter cassava, for lack of a bandage, closed up

our wounds!
Shit!
We were going to found a country
    that was shared among all of us,
not just the landholders list on this island!
Open to all of the islands,
to all of the blacks! All the blacks of the world!
But then came the procurators,
dividing the house,
laying their hands on our mother,
debasing her, in the eyes of the world,
to a trivial, contemptible puppet!
Christophe! Pétion!
I turn my back on this double tyranny,
that of the brute,
of the sneering skeptic—
who knows which side does more harm?
Great promised land,
to salute you with a man's salute
we have kept watch on the crests of the *mornes,*
in the hollows of the ravines. Kept watch
on this black soil we stand on, reddening it
with our peasants' blood, to follow, instead of a king,
the hypnotic spell of the imperious conch.
Now, O Death,
I want to fall like a dream
in exile. And I'll give no thanks for a respite.

MAGNY [*to the officer*]: Proceed! Grant the poor devil his wish
    and finish him off!

[*The officer fires and Metellus dies. In another part of the battlefield,
amid flags, drums, and trumpets, Christophe stands, surrounded by
a group of officers.*]

CHRISTOPHE: A bitter day! Many men have fallen! Some important parts of our country also, alas! Alas, poor face, much torn by our nails! Drouillard, Garesché, Deschezelles, such beautiful scars of good farmland, yes, and harvests like none we've seen, now just a scrap of blessed bread from our Haitian earth. See the well-curbs hemmed in by brambles, the burned fragments of walls amid wild banana-tree thickets, the cacti piercing, with heads like an armored fish, the dry wave of acacias.

And then the smell! Take a whiff of that!
I am no sailor,
But I imagine that from afar, Haiti
Must smell like that, Haiti
In the nostrils
Of the discoverer:
That odor of dried blood that scrapes your throat,
That smoke,
That intoxicant moisture,
That smell of burnt offerings refused by the gods!
But all's well: these are the final moments—
Come tomorrow, and that will be that!

[*Drawing on the ground a general's cocked hat*] The only thing left to do is to give Pétion back his hat, since he didn't have time to pick it up himself!

[*Laughter of officers. Hurrah from the soldiers. Trumpets. They exit.*]

SCENE 6

[*Civil war. Outside the besieged Port-au-Prince. Christophe's tent.*]

CHRISTOPHE:
Vastey, on the land there is nothing

But dust, over everything
Rubble,
Earth and thatch, crumbling mud-wall.
I want stone, give me stone!
And cement, bring me cement!
Everything's falling apart—oh, to set all this upright,
Upright in the face of the world, and solid!

[*The aides-de-camp come and go.*]

MAGNY: Sire, excuse me, but we are waiting to start the assault, and the troops are getting impatient.

CHRISTOPHE: Forget that, Magny.

MAGNY: But Sire, we've never had a more perfect opportunity! Pétion is at bay! Embrace your good fortune!

CHRISTOPHE: Forget it, I tell you. There won't be an assault. I've abandoned my whole campaign plan, starting with the siege of that town. I've dispatched an emissary to Pétion. I hope he will recognize that the moment has come to end our quarrel in order to build the country and unite this people against a danger, nearer than we had supposed, that could threaten its very existence!

MAGNY: This beggars belief! Such a union is unthinkable. We must beat them or be beaten. Excuse me if I insist.

CHRISTOPHE: You had better believe it, Magny, and if you need someone to initiate you in the faith, that would be *me!* I have spoken! Go!

MAGNY: And you—may your eyes not teach you too late!

[*Semidarkness, then light. The scene is Port-au-Prince, in the senate of the republic. A most parliamentary atmosphere, a parodic style.*]

THE LEADER OF THE OPPOSITION: My dear colleagues, upon to hear that which we are now hearing, I cannot refrain from sharing with this assembly something of the painful impression that I am suffering from. Yes, good sirs, there is one thing of which I am sure, of which we are all sure: and that is that the monarchy of Christophe is a mockery. But then I am led to ask myself whether we have done any better, whether our own republic is anything more than a mockery of a republic and our parliament more than a mockery of a parliament. Mr. President, it falls to your lot to persuade us: the assembly has the right to know, and it is your duty to tell us all. Why these circumlocutions? Why such secrecy? What are you up to? What are you plotting behind the back of the nation?

PÉTION: I accept the battle that the opposition has offered (for it is our pride that we tolerate an opposition!) on the very ground where it has so unfortunately chosen to wage it. I do not intend to hide anything from the assembly, still less to impose unduly upon its free decision. I am a democrat, and I wish to be not the commander but rather the guide of our free nation. Therefore, the nation shall know all my thoughts; it is the nation that will decide, and when the nation has decided, I assure you, Pétion will take action!

THE LEADER OF THE OPPOSITION: But speak! Speak! Explain yourself! What exactly does General Christophe want? What does he demand? That we recognize him as our head of state? And on what grounds does he base his claim? On all the innocent blood he has shed?

[*Applause.*]

PÉTION: If the opposition (and it is our glory that we here in this body tolerate an opposition), if the opposition had been guided less by the spirit of haste and perverse distrust and more by the spirit of measured prudence and probity that should always inspire legislators of our free republic, then, sirs, no one would—to the greatest joy of our enemies—have troubled this hour of national solidarity with such vain quarreling.

Indeed, Christophe proposes the reunification of the island. It goes without saying that it would be under his authority, his royal munificence deigning, no doubt, to distribute among you and me some paltry rewards, the stipends of low-level sinecures. In short, we would become the subjects of His Most Christophean Majesty!

A REPRESENTATIVE: That's outrageous!

A REPRESENTATIVE: No deals with that tyrant!

A REPRESENTATIVE: That puffed-up pasha!

A REPRESENTATIVE: Better Louis XVIII than Christophe!

A REPRESENTATIVE: May Heaven take vengeance upon him!

[*The lights go out. When they come on, the scene is again the tent of Christophe before Port-au-Prince, filled with officers, aides de camp.*]

MAGNY: Well, sir, now you know!

CHRISTOPHE: Poor Africa! Or rather, poor Haiti! It's the same thing anyway. Back there, the tribes, the languages, rivers, castes, forests, town against town, village against village.

Here, blacks, mulattoes, quadroons, obeah-men, God-knows-what, clan, caste, color, distrust and rivalry, cockfights, dogfights over a bone, louse-fights!

[*Roaring.*]

Dust! Dust! Dust everywhere! No stone, only dust! Only shit and dust!

[*Calmly*] Say, Magny, order the troops to march. To the Cape! To the North! Forward march!

HUGONIN [*playing the busybody*]: Hallo, comrades! We're turning about. With or without a bite to eat, we'll caper off to the Cape. As the king says: a louse-fight!

[*Sings*]

> *A louse and a flea*
> *On a stool once sat,*
> *And while playing cards*
> *They got into a spat.*
> *The flea pulled his hair,*
> *It was all she could do,*
> *And she said you old fool,*
> *You lousy for true!*

CHRISTOPHE: Now's a fine time to sing, Hugonin!

[*To Vastey*] You see, Vastey, the human material needs recasting. But how? I don't know. We'll do what we can in our nook of the world. In our little workshop! The smallest county in the universe is immense, if the hand is broad and the will does not falter. Forward march!

[*They exit. Fanfare.*]

SCENE 7

[*Christophe's villa. Banquet for the anniversary of the coronation. Christophe and his entourage.*]

CHRISTOPHE [*relaxed*]: I hear that in France the celebration was done the same day as the coronation.

THE MASTER OF CEREMONIES: Yes, Your Majesty. [*Pompous and technical*] At Rheims, in the great hall of the Archbishop, or the Tau Palace, in the presence of all the dignitaries, with the Master of the King's Store bearing the casket of His Majesty.

CHRISTOPHE: The casket! How very odd!

THE MASTER OF CEREMONIES: That is, a chest for the silverware. And that great cup-bearer, the saucer.

CHRISTOPHE: The saucer, you say?

THE MASTER OF CEREMONIES: The saucer, the glassware and decanter of His Majesty, the great carving-knife, the great spoon and the great knife of His Majesty. Everyone dressed and mantled in black velour lined with gold; I would add that a rostrum is set up for the queen and the princesses . . .

CHRISTOPHE: How strange! Ah well, if not the queen, at least Madame Christophe is here—not up on a dais, but among us, beside us, which is better. Tough luck for tradition! Today my cup-bearer will pour no wine, my carver will carve no meat.

HUGONIN: Your Majesty, what you're saying cleaves my heart and pierces my throat.

[*Singing*]

> *This one plucks me*
> *This one cooks me*
> *This one eats up all*
> *The little one gets nothing*

Lick the plate, my friend
Lick the plate . . .

CHRISTOPHE: Rest assured, gentlemen, you will not serve, but you shall be served.

HUGONIN: That's good! I breathe again! You restore my life, Your Majesty. My life and my appetite.

CHRISTOPHE [*to* THE MASTER OF CEREMONIES]: Indeed, I hate nothing so much as servile imitation . . . I think, Mr. Master of Ceremonies, that if we are to raise this people to civilization (and none has done more for that cause than I), we must also let the national spirit speak. And that's why we're gathered so informally, Haitian-style, not in the Salle du Tau as you said but on the veranda, dare I say, of our tropical hut, drinking not champagne but three-star Barbancourt, the best clairin of Haiti.

CHANLATTE [*reciting*]: How sweet the weeping reeds upon the plains . . .

CHRISTOPHE: What is that, Chanlatte? In the midst of our cheerful banquet, what does this sniveling mean, this plaintive weeping?

CHANLATTE: Nothing, Your Majesty, just a poem to the glory of rum, understood as our national drink.

CHRISTOPHE: National . . . national drink. Very interesting. Sing that again.

CHANLATTE:
How sweet the reeds upon these yell'wing plains!
Afar, a hundred presses groan their pains!
Th'ambrosial sap, from mingled canes squeezed dry,
Transformed to sugar, greets th'admiring eye,

Or, bubbling slowly, in a frothy lace
It rises, trembles, and o'erflows my glass.

CHRISTOPHE: No doubt about it, that's about rum. Well done, Chanlatte, it's very national, and we'll have it taught in our schools.

HUGONIN: Now what? No more beer? No more champagne? Believe me, I'm as patriotic as anyone else. Anti-white as anyone else, but I must admit that champagne is . . .

CHRISTOPHE: By thunder! Do we or do we not want a national poetry? Champagne, champagne, you worthless guzzler! Here, to help you forget champagne, catch this! Enjoy yourself!

[*He throws him a morsel as if to a dog.*]

HUGONIN [*barking*]: Thank you, thank you, Papa!

CHRISTOPHE: Eat first, you will thank me later. And you, Bishop, speak. Speak, all of you! Like children on New Year's Eve, let each of you, at the dawn of this reign and this banquet's end, pay your compliments.

CORNEILLE BRELLE: I say that you have placed a good cornerstone and built a fine house. May the Lord enlarge it further, and bring to it strength and comfort.

CHRISTOPHE [*laughing*]: Yeah, yeah—old frock-hanger, when you talk to the Lord, you do it in Latin!

CORNEILLE BRELLE: Oh, if it pleases Your Majesty! If you wish it! I am no part-time country priest.

[*Reciting*]

Mane surgens Jacob erigebat lapidem
intitulum, fundens oleum desuper
votum vovit Domino
Nisi Dominus aedificaverit domum in vanum
laboraverunt qui aedificant eam.
Nisi Dominus custodierit civitatem, frustra
vigilat qui custodit eam.

CHRISTOPHE: *Amen!* But say, Chanlatte, aren't you jealous? To spout this little sermon, Brelle rides in on the finest horse in his ecclesiastical stable. And your own muse, still stumbling and shying, drags behind like an old nag.

CHANLATTE: No, not at all! Soldierly and patriotic! National and lyrical! Such is my muse, O king. Ready at the first order! Fit as a fiddle. It is the Amazon of the King of Dahomey!

CHRISTOPHE: So much the better! Now there's a fine calling card!

CHANLATTE [*declaiming*]:
What accents suddenly have charmed my ear
And with what harmonies, transports sincere,
Have these our latitudes been favorèd?
Do we yet wake, or has some dream's deceit
Or suasions of some glozing untruth sweet
Bewitched our senses and becalmed our minds?
The honest warrior the throne inherits,
The prize of a great heart, both pure and loyal;
Fate ever smiles upon the man of merits
Who saves his realm with touch of mantle royal.

CHRISTOPHE: He doesn't touch it, Chanlatte—he *wears* it, and by acknowledged right! Never mind—Ow! Ow! Who's biting my leg?

HUGONIN [*coming out from under the table*]: Bow-wow-wow! I wish to say that I am His Majesty's dog, his pug, his lapdog, his mastiff, his bulldog!

CHRISTOPHE: A compliment that bites my calf! Go lie down, you spawn of an imbecile!

PRÉZEAU: A message, Your Majesty. A letter from London, delivered by way of Sir Alexis Popham.

CHRISTOPHE: My noble friend Wilberforce! Felicitations on the anniversary of my coronation. Ha . . . he writes that he has enrolled me in several scientific societies, as well as the Bible Society of England!

[*Laughter.*]

How's that, Archbishop? Can that do any harm? But Wilberforce, you teach me nothing, and you are not the only one to reason thus: "*One does not invent a tree, one plants it! One does not extract its fruits, but allows it to bear them. A nation is not a creation, but rather a gradual ripening, year by year, ring by ring.*" Well, isn't that good! Be prudent! *Sow*, he tells me, *sow the seeds of civilization.* Right. But unfortunately, those grow damned slowly.

We must give time due time. But we don't have time to wait when it's precisely time that has us by the throat! To entrust the fate of a people to sun, rain, and the seasons, what a strange idea!

MADAME CHRISTOPHE: Christophe!
I am nothing but a poor woman, I
Who served, though I'm now queen,
At the Inn of the Crown!
A crown on my head won't make me anything else
Than the simple woman,

The good black woman, who tells her husband:
"Beware!"
Beware, Christophe, of putting the roof of one house
On top of another—
It will fall through, or it will be too big.
Christophe, don't demand too much of men,
And too much of yourself!
Besides, I'm a mother,
And sometimes when I see you spurring the fiery
Horse of your heart,
My own heart
Falters, and I say to myself:
Let's hope we won't measure
The children's misery by their father's excess!
Our children, Christophe, think of our children.
My God! How will all of this end?

CHRISTOPHE: I demand too much of men! But not enough of
black folks, Madame. If there's anything that irritates me
as much as the talk of pro-slavery hacks, it's hearing our
philanthropists cry, no doubt with the best of intentions,
that all men are men and that there's no such thing as
whites and blacks. That's idle thinking, cut off from the
world, Madame. All men have the same rights. That I affirm. But of our common kind, some have more responsi-
bilities than others. There is the inequality. An inequality
of demands, do you understand? Who will have us believe
that all men, I say all, without privilege, without special
exemption, have known deportation, trafficking, slavery,
collective debasement to the status of beasts, total outrage,
enormous insult, which all who have suffered it wear, plas-
tered over their bodies, their faces: the all-annihilating
spit! We alone, Madame, you understand, we alone, we
blacks! Plunged, then, in the depths of the ditch! Oh yes,

I understand well: in the lowest depths of the ditch. It is there that we cry out; from there we aspire to the air, the light, the sun. And if we want to climb out again, see what demands that lays on us—the foot arching, the muscles straining, teeth that can grip and hold! And the head, oh, the head, capacious and cool. And therefore one must demand more of blacks than of others: more work, more faith, more enthusiasm, a step, another step, and yet one more step, and to keep what is gained with each step! It's of a resurgence never yet seen that I speak, good sirs, and woe to him whose foot slides back!

MADAME CHRISTOPHE: A king indeed.
Christophe, do you know how, in my little
Woolly head, I think of a king?
I'll tell you! In the midst of savannahs ravaged
By spiteful sun, he's the full and vigorous leaves
Of the great mombin tree, under which
Cattle, thirsting for shadow, take refuge.
But you? But you?
Sometimes I ask myself—
Because you try to do everything,
To control everything—if you aren't instead
The great fig tree that takes all the plants
Growing around it and strangles them!

CHRISTOPHE: That is called the "Accursed Fig Tree."
Think about it, dear wife!
Ah! I demand too much of blacks?
[*Leaping up*] There! Listen! Somewhere in the night, the tam-tam beats. Somewhere in the night, my people dance. And it's like that every day as well. Every day . . . every night . . . The ocelot is in the bush, the prowler is at our door, the man-hunter lying in wait, with his rifle, his snare, and his muzzle; the trap is set, the crime of our per-

secutors bites at our heels all around us, and my people dance!

[*Imploring*] But who,
Who then,
Will offer me
More than a priest's litany, more than praises in verse, more than parasitical flattery, more than a woman's caution,
Something, I say, that will set this people
to work,
something to educate
rather than *edify* this people?

Say there, Prézeau, send me Martial Besse. And you, you bunch of slackers and guzzlers: what are you waiting for, why don't you go out dancing as well? Get the hell out of here! I said get the hell out! No women, no priests, no courtiers . . . Don't you hear me? Get the hell out, God damn it! I, the king, shall keep watch alone.

MARTIAL BESSE: Here I am, Your Majesty.

CHRISTOPHE: What, Martial, nothing? No idea, no proposition?

MARTIAL BESSE: Your Majesty, to create for a people its patrimony,
its own unique patrimony
of beauty, strength, and confidence,
I can think of no achievement more worthy of
the people's advocate than that which calls them
to strive to their limit,
awakening them to their own hidden power!

CHRISTOPHE: Thank you, Martial Besse . . . thank you . . . I'll keep your idea: a patrimony. And in addition I say a patrimony of energy and pride. Of pride, why not? Consider the swelling breast of the earth, the earth that contracts and expands, breaking loose from its sleep, the first step out of chaos, the first stride of the sky!

MARTIAL BESSE: Your Majesty, those are frightfully steep slopes to build on!

CHRISTOPHE: Precisely—this people must claim for itself, must will and succeed at, something impossible! Against fate, against history, against Nature! Ah, ah! Unheard-of attack by our bare hands! Borne by our wounded hands, our wild defiance! On this mountain, the precious cornerstone, the firm foundation, the well-tried monolith. Assault of heaven or sun's dwelling-place, I don't know . . . the first charge of the morning watch! Look, Besse: imagine, on this unlikely platform, turned toward magnetic north, one hundred-thirty feet high, twenty feet thick in the walls, of limestone and the ashes of cane trash, limestone and bulls' blood: a citadel. Not a palace. Not a strong-house to protect my goods. I say the Citadel, the liberty of all the people. Built by the whole people, men and women, children and elders, built for the whole people! See how its head dreams toward the clouds, its feet plumb the abyss, while its mouths spit grapeshot as far as the open sea and the hollows of valleys; it is a city, a fortress, a massive breast-plate of stone! Impregnable, Besse, impregnable! Yes, Mr. Engineer, to each people its monuments! For this people forced to its knees, a monument that will set it upright! Right here! Rising! Watching!

[*Hallucinating*] Ah, look! Don't you see that it lives? It sounds its charge through the fog. Its lights blaze at nightfall! It cancels the slave ship! Vast procession on horseback! My friends, who have drunk bitter salt and the dark wine of the sand, both I and you thrown down by the heavy swell, I have seen the enigmatic prow, with spray and blood in its nostrils, beat through the wave of contempt!

May my people, my black people,
Salute the fragrance and flood tide of the future!

[*An image of the Citadel appears, clearly seen in the distance, illuminated in the night beyond a double range of mountains.*]

END OF ACT I

INTERLUDE

THE COMMENTATOR: Can you stop a country from crying out?
From Môle Saint Nicolas in the North to Jérémie in the South.

Haiti is a big mouth, and the language of Haiti, the passage that comes from afar, its deepest gash in the midst of its highlands, the living trench where its most intimate speech and most secret blood mix, invents an immortal name: The Artibonite. And if I return (Honor! Respect!), it is to speak to you of the river Artibonite, the father-river of Haiti, as King Christophe says.

The generous friend! How he creates by himself new arms, false arms, channels, lagoons, as though to help everyone out. And for youthful vigor no one can match him! Fragments of epic, of gods, goddesses, sirens, the hope and despair of a people, the anguish of high plateaus and the savannah, the violence and tenderness of a people, the river Artibonite, in his capacious, capricious pouring-forth of lacelets of eddies on lacelets of eddies, carries and carries away, transports, pours and divulges all, from the high Dominican mountains to—it's useless to search the map—it is known as the Great Salty. (It is wing upon wing of the solemn flight of pink flamingos at twilight; also a racket of wild pigs in the confusion of mangroves; a rocking cradle of manchineel and hopbush.)

. . . And he carries also, in due season, the enormous tree-trunks bound together as rafts, made of the logwood the river feeds from its ooze. Fifty meters square at the surface, weighing ten tons, the whole floating half-immersed on a frame of bamboo and the buoyant trunks of bananas, these Kon-Tikis are not easy to steer. And the job's not easy of those who ride them and who are known here as "raft-keepers." No sail. No rudder. And that means the raft-keepers, leaning heavily on their large perches of mango-trees, have time to sing, tell stories, or ponder philosophy.

[*Vision of the river Artibonite; enormous wood convoys steered by the raft-keepers.*]

APPRENTICE RAFT-KEEPER [*singing*]:
Aguay rooh-oh!
Aguay rooh-oh!
Two months since we set off, that's a long time going down a river.

RAFT-KEEPER CAPTAIN: Long.

APPRENTICE RAFT-KEEPER: When do we get to the sea?

RAFT-KEEPER CAPTAIN: The Great Salty? It won't be long.

APPRENTICE RAFT-KEEPER: All the same, it *is* long!

RAFT-KEEPER CAPTAIN: The big truth is not in the going, but knowing which way to go.

APPRENTICE RAFT-KEEPER, *singing*:
Aguay rooh-oh!
Master Aguay
Don't leave—that boat

Go capsize
Aguay oh!

[*The raft-keepers lean on their perches. The rafts advance ponderously.*]

RAFT-KEEPER CAPTAIN [*blowing his conch shell*]: That means, raft-keepers, attention! The mouth of the Great Salty is not far. Hey kid, you too—pay attention!

APPRENTICE RAFT-KEEPER: But we're already there!

RAFT-KEEPER CAPTAIN: Well, it's there that we have to push hardest. And we got no choice. On the Great Salty, someone will throw you a rope. If you catch it, that's fine, you'll reach land and moor there. If you fail, God help you! Then all you can do is throw yourself in the arms of Mama Water.

APPRENTICE RAFT-KEEPER: And the raft?

RAFT-KEEPER CAPTAIN: In that case, it's "good-bye, raft!" The logwoods drift out to sea. The sea devours them and spits them back. On the other shore, they say, where the whites of America live, though I never been there to see them.

APPRENTICE RAFT-KEEPER: Funny job, this!

RAFT-KEEPER CAPTAIN: You have to know how to spur the beast. And how to put on the harness. It's not a job, it is life itself.

APPRENTICE RAFT-KEEPER:
Aguay, Aguay! Rooh!

RAFT-KEEPER CAPTAIN [*singing and straining on his perch*]:
Aguay, Rooh—oh!
Aguay roio—oh!
Don't leave—that boat go capsize!
Don't leave—that country go capsize!

ACT II

[Haitian countryside. A field. It's rest time for the peasants.]

SCENE 1

FIRST PEASANT: Here—this water cool, it come from the river that run through the red apple trees.

SECOND PEASANT: Thanks. Yes, it cool, but a touch of clairin wouldn't be bad either. Nothing like a bit of dry clairin to beat the fatigue when you work up a sweat. The best pick-me-up.

FIRST PEASANT: Well, friend, it going to rain. And it won't rain clairin. Look: Morne Bédoret steaming, and when you see mist on Bédoret, bad weather coming. Every time. All the same, is damned pretty country: coffee trees, cocoa trees, and this water that run through the red apple trees and the bamboo trees.

SECOND PEASANT: Yes, friend. I wouldn't say different. The country beautiful, oh yes . . . but not the climate, this time we living in.

FIRST PEASANT: There are things you don't say, friend. The time neither good nor bad. The taste is all in the mouth. Is the way you take it make it taste good or bad.

SECOND PEASANT: Believe me, friend: it have some people won't let you take the time. They shove it down the back of your throat like medicine.

FIRST PEASANT: Well, you can't say it have anything wrong with a good dose of bush medicine to revive you.

SECOND PEASANT: I wouldn't-a say anything bad if it was a good dose of bush medicine that did do me some good. But I say to myself: when we beat the whites back into the sea, that was to have this land for ourselves, not to toil on the land of others, even if they are black, but to have it for ourselves like a wife, no?

FIRST PEASANT: Friend, you don't have to turn rebel: I myself say sometimes that Christophe is too fond of the stick. But being too fond of the stick don't make a man a bad father and husband. Bah! If you want my opinion, Pétion is a fella who allow everything and just let the grain grow. He like a mother who spoil her son to spite the father. But a father is a father, and if he hard, is for the good of his son, and because he proud of his son. Think about that, old friend, think about that.

SECOND PEASANT: Friend, when I think of all that, is not pride that's needed . . . is understanding.

FIRST PEASANT: God is good. You must trust in Him.

SECOND PEASANT: God is good. But far above us. The trouble is getting the prayer up to Him. Ha, ha! With the damned Royal Dahomeyans, there's no way to worship the *lwa*. As soon as the drums start beating, they come down on us, plakata, plakata, plakata. You'd start to think it ent have no more freedom for gods than it have for men.

FIRST PEASANT: Friend, excuse me, excuse me . . .

[*Horses galloping.*]

SECOND PEASANT: What I just tell you? Plakata, plakata, plakata! Is the Royal. We in a fine mess now!

[*The Royal Dahomeyans pass. The peasants ostentatiously set to work. The division of Royal Dahomeyans stops uphill of the peasants. Their captain reads a proclamation. His voice, punctuated by drumrolls, grows louder and louder, to the point of obsession.*]

THE ROYAL DAHOMEYAN [*reading*]: "And so that my proclamation should be executed in full, and that all the abuses that have crept in among the cultivators should cease from the moment of proclamation of this decree, I issue the following strict orders:

"Article 1—All managers, drovers, and cultivators must fulfill their duties, with precision, submission, and obedience—as soldiers do.

"Article 2—All managers, drovers, and cultivators who do not assiduously discharge their duties, laid upon them by agriculture, shall be arrested and punished with the same severity as soldiers who fail in theirs.

"Article 3—The generals and superior officers are charged with supervising the execution of this present decree, for which I will hold them personally responsible. I would like to believe that their devoted support of my pursuit of our public prosperity will continue, convinced as they are that *liberty cannot exist without labor.*

"Signed: Christophe."

[Drumrolls. The peasants, momentarily stunned, return to their work.]

PEASANTS [*singing*]:
    A-go, the handle come off my hoe.
    Boys, if the handle gone
    We go put it back on.
    A-go! A-go!

SCENE 2

[At Cape Henry. A bourgeois drawing room.]

FIRST LADY: My dear, have you heard the latest? It's fine news indeed and concerns our sex. Would you believe that he's mobilized the royal family? Including the girls. And from now on, Athenaïs and Amethyst, the princesses as we call them, are ordered to go to the stoneyards at least once a week. The princesses!

SECOND LADY: And to do what, I ask you? Handle food supplies?

FIRST LADY: You'll never guess! One's going to display the flag, and the other will lend her voice to revive the failing courage of the workers. They've even cooked up some titles: from now on, there'll be a Flag-Queen and a Singing-Queen. Well—what do you say?

SECOND LADY: Alas, my own story is even sadder. It's the story of a poor man. It seems he was sleeping on his veranda at an unsuitable hour. I mean an hour not approved by the Code Henry. The king saw him from a high wall on the Citadel, through his field glasses. O my stars, what rage! He calls an officer. They go into the artillery hall. You can imagine the rest.

[*In a corner of the stage, we see a flashback of the narrated scene.*]

CHRISTOPHE: *There—look at that! Look, I tell you! General Guerrier . . . what did you see?*

GUERRIER: *A poor peasant. Exhausted, no doubt.*

CHRISTOPHE: *Exhausted! . . . General! Battery Twelve in position! Aim! Fire!*

GUERRIER: *Fire!*

HUGONIN: *Oh, la la! The hut in a blaze! The poor fellow pulped! Bravo, Your Majesty, for the Royal Artillery. Sensitive souls, don't feel too sorry for him! He's passed from the little sleep to the Big Sleep without knowing what hit him!* Requiescat in pace!

FIRST LADY: How horrible! How horrible! But here's Mr. Vastey. Baron, you are welcome.

VASTEY: I kiss your hands, Madam.

SECOND LADY: I'm delighted to see you, Mr. Vastey. But you've made yourself scarce since you took on the burdens of statecraft.

VASTEY: Let all that be, Madame.

SECOND LADY: But we can't, we aren't given a choice. Mr. Vastey, once upon a time, there was a king, full of violent humors. And his subjects wondered whether . . .

VASTEY: No, Madam! Contemplated instead the beautiful, the rare spectacle of a great force set in motion—enraged, no doubt, but a force.

FIRST LADY: A force? My God, I hadn't thought of that. A force? But then, what do we expect from it but that it will crush us?

VASTEY: I expect of it, Madame, that it will affirm us, and first of all in our own eyes.

SECOND LADY: Well, in the meanwhile, it looks horribly like the same old thing that you, to your honor, once fought against. Once.

VASTEY: Eh. Well, sometimes history can go forward by only one road. And all must take it.

FIRST LADY: So the path of liberty and the path of slavery would be one and the same.

SECOND LADY: A charming paradox! In effect, King Christophe would serve liberty by the means of servitude!

VASTEY: And if it were proved that, well spent, the Devil's money could become the money of God? My own God, Madam, is the greatness of the state and the liberty of black people.

FIRST LADY: I see, Mr. Vastey, that I can never prevail in argument against such a lawyer as yourself. It's just as well; enough of politics! Isabelle, go to the harpsichord. She has a ravishing voice, that child. Isabelle, sing us that pretty ballad, the ballad of Ourika.

VASTEY: And who is this charming child, Ourika?

FIRST LADY: The heroine of a novel that brought all of Paris to tears. It's the story of a little black girl raised in Europe by a noble white family, who suffers for her color and dies because of it.

VASTEY: Ah! Interesting! Most interesting!

ISABELLE [*singing*]:
Child of black Guinea born,
Flower of that burning, distant sky,

Ourika, as she sat forlorn,
Cried out against her destiny.

France, that first my spirit moved
And welcomed, once, my wild transports,
You only hid me in your skirts:
I never, never shall be loved.

O color white, angelic white,
Of white my soul would worthy be.
Lord, I shall praise Thee day and night,
If Thou but grant this wish for me!

No, for oblivion you have bred
Ourika, by her fate betrayed:
Far better were it to be dead
Than languish as an unloved maid.

FIRST LADY: Bravo! Bravo! I could die! What do you think, Mr. Vastey?

VASTEY: I think of Christophe, Madame. Do you know why he's working day and night? You know, his violent humors, as you say, this frenzied work? . . . It's so that never again, anywhere in the world, shall there be a young black woman ashamed of the color of her skin, who finds her color an obstacle to realizing the wishes of her heart.

SCENE 3

CHRISTOPHE: For the Citadel, we've got to do more and do it faster. It should be possible to draw on the better part of all the labor force of the country, and I mean all: women and children too.

VASTEY: And children?

CHRISTOPHE: Yes, children. The little bastards! It's their future we're building! The rampart without which the falcon would be permitted to steal its prey the second he sees it; the trellis for the fragile, newly blossomed tree! So: everyone to work, to serve, to transport the stones. Ten stones a day for the women, that wouldn't kill them, no? Two to five per child, according to age. Where is Prézeau?

PRÉZEAU: Here I am, Sire.

CHRISTOPHE: I charge you, Prézeau, with settling the Basin affair. I made him Count of Retting Mountain and gave him Deschappelles as his fiefdom, and now I learn that he is whipping the peasants! What's going on? I put workers at his disposal, I didn't give him slaves. Send a division of the Royal Dahomeyans down there. Have the slave-driving manager tied to a tree, in a public place, in front of all of the people. And have him cut apart with a saber, limb by limb.

As for Basin, tell him I say he must come here tomorrow. We'll never have enough workmen for the Citadel.

It's time to talk sense into those blacks who think the Revolution means taking the place of the whites, yet continuing in the same way—that is, on the backs of us blacks—to play the white man.

Prézeau, I want you to have a few words—and I mean strong words—with the director of the stud farm at the Bronze Pasture. Tell Rigolo Socrate, for that's his name, that I'll stand for no rigmarole. He writes to me that one of my English stallions is dead. Send him word for once and for all that Socrates is a man, ergo mortal; that my horses are not men; that they may shed their coat, but they do not die. On this understanding, I grant him a period of three months to replace the beast. Otherwise, I'll take my saber to him in front of his own stud-horse.

And as for you, Richard, we have an account to settle.

RICHARD: With me, Your Majesty?

CHRISTOPHE: With you, Richard! And I'll tell you a story that you already know. The Emperor Dessalines was given a dancing master who invented, in his honor, the Carabinier.

HUGONIN [*singing in a grotesque manner*]:
The Emperor come to see the cuckoo,
Emperor dance away.
Requiescat in pace!

CHRISTOPHE: Shut up, Hugonin! The dancing master was named Manuel. Hugonin is right: at my accession, I had him put to death. He debased the nation and made its king ridiculous.

RICHARD: Your Majesty, I confess I don't see how that's relevant.

HUGONIN: Your Majesty, he says he can't see how that's relevant.
The Emperor come to see, cuckoo,
Emperor dance away!

CHRISTOPHE: Cut it out, Hugonin! Richard, since I have to spell it out for you, you comported yourself in a ridiculous manner at the ball yesterday evening. So now can you see the connection? Know that I am displeased when my nobility lowers itself to buffoonery. In my court, one does not dance the *bamboula*, good sir. Do you understand at last? You will leave this evening for Thomasico, with the rank of captain.

RICHARD: Of captain? To that grubby little town at the edge of the kingdom?

CHRISTOPHE: Precisely—it suits you. There you can dance the Carabinier whenever you please.

HUGONIN:

The Emperor went to see, cuckoo,
Emperor dance away!

CHRISTOPHE: Obviously, good sirs, affairs are tending toward a point at which, if I do not take care, anarchy may steal into my kingdom.

MAGNY: Anarchy?

CHRISTOPHE: I say: A-nar-chy! If the cap fits, wear it!
Ah, what a job: to set a people upright! And here am I, like a schoolmaster brandishing his rod at a nation of dunces! Sirs, understand well what these decisions mean. Either everything breaks, or all will be set upright! That it all might break is conceivable . . . All over the place, a bare nakedness. Well, that's a freedom like any other. The land remains: the stars, the night, and we, the blacks, with freedom, edible roots, wild banana trees. It's an idea. Or else we put things upright! And you know the rest: then we have to keep at it, to carry the weight, higher and higher. Farther and farther. I, for my part, have chosen: we have to bear up. We have to march on. And that's why, Brelle [*the archbishop is startled*]—yes, I've a bone to pick with you, Archbishop—I must say that I don't appreciate your request to go back to France. I have made you Duke of l'Anse; I have built you the most beautiful archbishop's palace in the New World, and now you think to abandon me and return to Europe!

BRELLE: Your Majesty, after twenty years in the tropics, I've earned the right to rest.

CHRISTOPHE: Rest! Rest! They've all got that word in their mouths! Even you, Brelle, my old comrade!

BRELLE: I have an old mother in France.

CHRISTOPHE: There is everything still to be done, Brelle!

BRELLE: Your throne is safe, the realm prospers, and you see before you an old priest exhausted by his evangelical labors, who can do nothing further.

CHRISTOPHE: What is this, Brelle? Having once begun, one does not abandon the task! Even to go embrace one's old mother. All right, all right . . . I'll think about it. Meanwhile, I have work for you . . . Hugonin, the peasants are here. Let that rabble come in!

[*Enter peasant men and women.*]

SCENE 4

CHRISTOPHE [*to the peasant men*]: Good sirs, I hear some pretty reports of you. The reports I've received say that you have not married, that you are a bunch of libertines!

HUGONIN: Yes, Your Majesty, the men philander right, philander left, without rhyme or reason. They're fornicators, Your Majesty. It's terrible! Fornicators!

CHRISTOPHE: Understood. You might as well say conspirators. Well, all that has to stop! Our state needs a stable keel, and no state is stable unless the family is stable! No family is stable unless women are stable! I don't want my subjects fooling around like that with their trousers down, like savages!
So I've decided to marry you all at once.
Hugonin, I put you in charge of public morality.

HUGONIN: Of public morality? I? Thank you, Your Majesty. Coming from you, my Prince, nothing could touch me more than this homage to my good character, my honesty, my morals, my virtue, my . . .

CHRISTOPHE: Yeah, yeah.

HUGONIN: Ladies and gentlemen, the king, in his fatherly solicitude, has decided to spare you the trouble of courting before you choose . . . Here you are, my children, all the men are here, all the women are here. To each his woman, to each her man . . . and vice versa. Let's see—will she do, that one there? Yes, wouldn't she? A little bit fat! But the fat ones are the best ones! She's yours . . . Sold! . . . For you, the little thin one! All right? There's someone for every taste . . . You, you've got a build like Hercules . . . And that woman there looks like she's got a strong back . . . By thunder, a back like that could throw an elephant into the air! So what are you waiting for? Take her . . . And serve yourselves!

Gentlemen! To each foot its own shoe . . .

Your Majesty, a woman like that is a gold mine. With her, you could father a regiment!

Come, ladies and gentlemen, agriculture needs hardworking arms, and the state needs soldiers . . .

Well then, I'll put it to you like this: good night, and plow hard!

CHRISTOPHE: Let's see . . . Brelle, give them your benediction. And note that we still have need of you . . . I bet this is the biggest marriage you've ever presided at, eh?

[*The archbishop blesses the crowd.*]

And now, France, let's settle the score.

[*Enter Vastey, who hands to Christophe a message from the king of France.*]

SCENE 5

VASTEY [*reading the address on a letter*]: "To the General Christophe, Commander of the Northern Province of Saint-Domingue."

CHRISTOPHE: Vastey, this can be nothing but a secretarial error. A . . . how do you say, a la . . . a lap . . .

VASTEY: A lapse, Your Majesty. A *lapsus calami.*

CHRISTOPHE: Very well then, yes, a lapse that escaped the secretary to the Secretary of Foreign Affairs of my cousin, the King of France. Fine. To each sin its mercy. Anyhow, this shouldn't prevent us from addressing the problem of what my good cousin calls "the question of Saint-Domingue." Let Mr. Franco de Médina come in.

FRANCO DE MÉDINA: As I have had the pleasure to affirm the order that reigns in this part of the island, I am now pleased to salute the great wisdom and high spirit of moderation of him that rules it with such talent and strength.

CHRISTOPHE: When you address yourself to me, Mr. Franco de Médina, you call me "Sire." You say "Your Majesty." That is, shall we say, a local custom, which is if not the appropriate usage, then at least the common usage to which the visitor is expected to conform. That said, there is nothing to prevent you from broaching your conception of "the question of Saint-Domingue."

FRANCO DE MÉDINA: Precisely, Your Majesty.

CHRISTOPHE: There you go! "Your Majesty." Already, you are Haitianized. Well then, I understand. Nothing remains but to make yourself understood to these gentlemen. Sirs, you understand, this is spelled out in the letter that Mr. Franco de Médina has delivered to me from his master the king. You understand that you are revolted slaves. You, Magny, Duke of Plaisance, you, Guerrier, Duke of l'Avancé, you, Brelle, Duke of l'Anse, you, Trou-Bonbon, you, Sale-Trou, you, Limonade, lieutenant-general of the king's armies, commander of the royal and military order of Saint-Henry, Secretary of State and Minister of Foreign Affairs, you understand that you are *maroons, escaped slaves,* and that the state of your king *is precarious.* The villain! The scoundrel! And I a king—to say such things to me, a king!

[*Suddenly very calm*] In short, Mr. Franco de Médina, what you are offering me is a deal. A deal made on the backs of my people! This free people would again put on its chains; our glorious army would lay down its arms to submit to the whip; the trophies they won on the field of battle would adorn their torturer's scaffold! And I, in the antechambers of your king, would wallow in gold-striped livery. In truth, sir, if you were not in a civilized country and protected by diplomatic immunity . . .

VASTEY: Allow me to remind His Majesty of that which will not have escaped him, that the envoy of the King of France, the agent of the King of France, as a native of the former Spanish portion of Saint-Domingue, now a province of Haiti, is clearly by law a Haitian, and therefore Your Majesty's subject.

CHRISTOPHE: Of course! Thank you, Vastey . . . thank you . . . I see that you were born to understand me and to serve me. Meanwhile, and to rule on "the problem of the question of Saint-Domingue," let it be known in France that, free by right and independent de facto, we will never renounce those advantages—no! That we will never permit the destruction of the edifice that we have raised with our own hands and cemented with our blood.

FRANCO DE MÉDINA: Your Majesty, understand me well, I come here bearing the olive branch . . .

CHRISTOPHE: You remember that, to my mind, most opportunely, Mr. Franco de Médina. Where is Prézeau?

PRÉZEAU: Here I am, Your Majesty.

CHRISTOPHE: Prézeau, have them beat the drums. Inform the people. You, Brelle, we have need of you. Even though he is a traitor, his soul has a right to its repose. You will see to that. And so that he may witness our zeal to do all that's necessary, while you officiate, Mr. Franco de Médina will stand next to his coffin and will hear his own requiem mass. After which, Gaffie, attention! These gentlemen are delicate. I don't want a single drop of blood to stain his jacket. Bon voyage, Mr. Franco de Médina!

SCENE 6

HUGONIN: Your Majesty, the Council of State is here, and the people too, all just burning to harangue you.

CHRISTOPHE: And what do these gentlemen want?

HUGONIN: I suppose they've come to say that they've had enough of eating wild plantain and watery mangoes.

[*Singing*]

One, two, three, four,
A bottle of wine awaits
All these good magistrates;
We've chocolates for
Each councilor;
Cassava for the peasantry,
And for the king, the evil eye.

VASTEY: Enough of your joking, Hugonin. But I think, Your Majesty, that the time has come to follow up on your idea of naming someone to deal with petitions, complaints, and grievances.

CHRISTOPHE: No point in that, Vastey. There is only one shepherd and only one flock. Let these gentlemen come in, I will receive them.

[*The delegations enter.*]

Sirs, I am pleased to see gathered here, in the person of their representatives from all the classes that together comprise the whole, our entire nation.

It's just as well; what I have to say to you concerns, precisely, the whole nation. Although the fear of war has passed, our problems and our tasks, within this peace, arise anew, and it is not leisure that I propose today, no, it is not leisure.

THE SPOKESMAN OF THE PEASANTS: Your Majesty, a canoe can stand the sea, but it's not always out in a storm. A silk-cotton tree can stand the wind, but it doesn't fight the wind every day. Your people are tired!

CHRISTOPHE: Old man, your crown of white hair entitles you to some tolerance, but, my good man, do not abuse it: you're setting out on a dangerous path!

And you, my Council of State—what? Not even the slightest remonstrance?

A COUNCILOR OF STATE: Your Majesty, the Council of State professes itself the true interpreter of our country in bringing you the tribute of its admiration for the peerless steadfastness that has been exercised in defense of the Haitian cause and of our liberty. On the basis of the unequivocally expressed sentiments of all our fellow citizens, it will make sure that the nation shall be recompensed for its long struggle and will open itself to the sweet hope that all classes of our society will finally enjoy, beneath the shelter of our tutelary arm, the rest that its heroic struggle and unflagging labors have merited.

CHRISTOPHE: The unflagging labors of the Council of State! Let's pretend I didn't hear that!

For all the good it's done, I would hate my victory at once if it encouraged you to be lax.

Who would awaken your stone of blackness,

To release, in its striking, your human sound?

Well, understand, I will give you no quittance! Tell me then, Councilor of State, you who are, supposedly, the memory of the realm, tell me, what was in this country before the coming of King Christophe? And what then was a Councilor of State?

A COUNCILOR OF STATE: Sire, there was no Councilor of State.

CHRISTOPHE: No and no again, there was no Councilor of State, only some burnt-necked niggers.

Repeat after me . . .

A COUNCILOR OF STATE: . . . some burnt-necked niggers, Your Majesty.

CHRISTOPHE: Not even that! There was shit, do you hear me, and nothing but shit!

Good! Gentlemen, the real issue is this: we are poor, and it's up to us to become rich; we are hungry and the land is there, needing only our arms and our willpower. Bahon, Vallières, Mont-Organisé, a fine reservation we've barely begun to develop. And the Artibonite, our national river. Rossignol-Lachicotte, Rossignol-des-Dunes, Rossignol-du-Lagon, once the finest cotton plantations on earth, now a ruin.

Do you understand: we must work again and rebuild everything. Everything: land and waters! Open new roads! Rework the land! Control the waters! Do you realize that the Artibonite—not our national river, no, I say our Father River—could be transformed to the Nile of Haiti? And you ask for rest? Do you believe that, since we have peace again, everyone can sprawl on his easy chair, and after his siesta, there on the porch of his daydreams, puff on his pipe between glasses of clairin?

A *raque*. You know what a *raque* is: the enormous crevasse, the endless trough through the mud. Specifically, on the banks of the Artibonite, you know the *raque of Maurapas*, packed thick with mud, unending, and this century is rain, a long march through endless rain. Yes, in the *raque*—we are in the *raque* of history.

For black people, getting through it means freedom. And, brother, too bad for you if you expect someone to lend you a hand! All right then, do you get me: you don't have the right to be tired! Go, gentlemen!

[*The delegations leave.*]

Wait a minute! I said "go," but not like that! Let's see . . . Bring shovels and pickaxes to these gentlemen. Coun-

cilor of State, shovel and pickax, on the right shoulder!
Let's go, let's go. Do it! Shovel! Pickax! One, two, one,
two! Forward march!

[*Exit the Council of State, bizarrely armed with agricultural tools.*]

THE PEASANT [*grumbling*]: Well, just between us, that's easy for
Nuncle to say. Funny idea, to go walk in the *raque*. You walk
alongside the *raque*. Everyone know that. The *raque* is a
trap. You better off taking the river—leave all the muck to
the left and right, cut through by the river. Nuncle, you'd
have to know the rivers.

CHRISTOPHE: What are you griping about, old man? Go away.
You see I've given you hands for your work!

[*The peasant withdraws, laughing.*]

SCENE 7

CHRISTOPHE: Prézeau!

PRÉZEAU: Here I am, Your Majesty!

CHRISTOPHE [*to himself*]:
    False words
    False lips
    Double heart
    Drooling tongue,
    Neck with no backbone!
    Men? Bah! Only shadows!
    My court is a theater of shadows!
    Yet I read on a slate all that is written

Under their thick skulls!
But where is Prézeau?

PRÉZEAU: Awaiting your orders, Majesty.

CHRISTOPHE: Ah! Uh . . . it's a matter concerning Brelle.
I have appointed him archbishop, but he has not been appointed by canon law! I have charged Péletier, who is in London—and who, it should be said as well, has cost me plenty in sugar and coffee—to deliver a message on that point to the pope. And the Holy Father has not replied! In short, Brelle is in an unauthorized position. It is very, very . . . tiresome, Prézeau! What do you think?

PRÉZEAU: Very, very tiresome, Your Majesty.

CHRISTOPHE: On that score, one may well ask if Brelle is truly the archbishop, eh, Prézeau?

PRÉZEAU: One might indeed wonder, Your Majesty.

CHRISTOPHE: Ah! It doesn't matter. My appointment counts more than the consecration of the pope. What's tiresome, Prézeau, is that Brelle has allowed himself to get old. He writes a lot. He talks a lot . . . much more than the welfare of the state requires.

PRÉZEAU: I am at your command, Your Majesty.

CHRISTOPHE: He's an old man, Prézeau, and an old comrade of mine.

PRÉZEAU: An old comrade, Your Majesty.

CHRISTOPHE: He talks too much, Prézeau. He writes too much. But no blood. No blood. A good death. In his own bed . . . He's an old man . . . gently . . . gently. Do it quickly, Prézeau!

[*Gradually louder and more quickly*] Have them wall up the doors and windows of the archbishop's palace. All of them—walled up completely. Leave nothing open, not even a cat door! Go! I shall give Brelle the finest archbishop's tomb of the New World!

SCENE 8

[*The Citadel. Pharaonic labors.*]

OVERSEER [*singing*]:
  Little ones, ol' ones,
  All them carts ol',
  All them bolos dull,
  All them oxen, no ho'ns,
  All them blacks in the mo'nes.
    Now what? No one sings the refrain? You don't want to work or what? Believe me, I'm telling you for your own good, that's for sure!

LABORERS [*singing, exhausted*]:
  We'll see about that.
  I runnin' away,
  Headin' home to my hut.

OVERSEER: This is a fine time to sing the leave-taking song. At any moment the Big Man could take us by surprise. Well, boys, I pity you!

LABORERS [*singing, exhausted*]:
  I runnin' away,
  I headin' home to my hut.

[*Enter Christophe and his entourage.*]

OVERSEER: Your Majesty, I must say that we can't keep it up in this weather. Maybe it's time to consider sending the workmen home. This wind could dehorn an ox.

CHRISTOPHE: You'll find that the oxen won't let themselves be dehorned. Look, I'm going to show you how a nigger of consequence works!

[*He picks up a trowel and sets to work.*]

LABORERS [*singing, exhausted*]:
   To make us eat that same old bread
   We won't be tricked again
   For nobody's pretty eyes
   From now on we refuse to die,
   From now on we won't die.

CHRISTOPHE: I don't like that tone! It's not about *dying.* It's about *doing,* do you understand?

[*Singing*]

   If the master's not so good,
   Still God is good
   Haiti is for the Haitians.

OVERSEER: Your Majesty, the difficulty is in hoisting the stones. The slope is steep and slippery: twelve degrees per meter. I have sent down a group of a hundred men. This has accomplished nothing.

CHRISTOPHE: Take out fifty from the ranks: that will help.

OVERSEER:
   Hoist up!
   Hoist up!

LABORERS [*singing*]:
> *Do not wash my head, Papa,*
> *Do not wash my head, Mama,*
> *When it's my sweat washes it, Papa,*
> *When it's the rain that soaks it.*

[*The weather has become worse and worse. Rain, lightning, and thunder.*]

CHRISTOPHE: It's a man who has fought a war who addresses you, and he assures you that it's no pleasure to be driven from *morne* to *morne*, from bush to bush. That's why I've decided to give my people this fine show of stones to rebuke all blows, this fine dog of stone whose mouth alone will discourage a pack of wolves.

HUGONIN: And if the French come all the same, they won't know what hit them! Tomatoes? Mangoes? Plums? No and no again! Fine cannonballs of iron in their bellies, Papa Christophe's best grapeshot and the roaring fires of confusion in their damned white asses!

[*Uproar of thunder and explosions. Spectacle of disorder.*]

CHRISTOPHE: But what is that? Eh? The lightning! Let's go, fellows. Let's not stop to gawk at these fireworks! Overseer, make the drums sound. Strike with all of your arms, breathe deeply with all your lungs: let the bamboo trumpet announce the cannon's thunder to thunder, let it be known that from now on we will speak with it eyebrow to eyebrow; the cymbal to answer lightning with lightning; the *lambi*, our visceral conch, to unleash against blind violence the still stronger violence of our breasts; loudly, and louder still, strike the small drum to unleash the rain, and tell the clouds we'll provoke their rage in order to rescue the sun!

AIDE DE CAMP: Your Majesty, the lightning has struck the gun-powder: the treasure-house is destroyed; the governor of the district and part of the garrison were swallowed up in the rubble.

CHRISTOPHE: Take heart, boys!
It's a battle like any other!
Agonglo!
The saw-toothed leaves
Gathered around the heart
Of the pineapple resist!
Thus the King of Dahomey salutes the future
Of his scepter's reign!
Is Fate is God—the lightning falls!
Agonglo: the pineapple resists!

[*He brandishes his sword against the sky.*]

Peter, saint we all adore,
Do you challenge us to war?

END OF ACT II

INTERLUDE

[*The Haitian countryside. A field at the end of the day. Some peasants at work with hoes and shovels.*]

FIRST PEASANT: Woy! Pierrot Patience, I talking to you, no?

SECOND PEASANT: Woy! Mr. Jupiter Taco.

FIRST PEASANT: I say we done enough of that work, and a little nip of refreshment wouldn't do any harm going down our throats.

SECOND PEASANT: And I say that's just the thing, brother Jupiter. I surprise I didn't hear the bell!

FIRST PEASANT: Bell or no bell, Mr. Patience. And whatever going on with the bell, I say maybe it have some broke-down machinery in this kingdom.

SECOND PEASANT: Sometimes, friend Jupiter, I wonder where you go looking to find this stuff you come up with. It wouldn't do for such words to fall on everybody ears.

FIRST PEASANT: Mr. Pierrot Patience, I'd say the Royal got other things to do than sniff around our talk. The Royal and the King too, harsh king as he is.

SECOND PEASANT: Things changing . . . Things changing. Tell me, you really believe in their freedom, the republic . . . all them pretty songs they singing?

FIRST PEASANT: Tell you for true, friend Patience, what I love is the earth. I believe in the earth that I work with my own arms, but the fat king won't put it in our arms to keep.

SECOND PEASANT: I hear that, bit by bit, he comin' around, he starting to give some plots for our own arms—our own army, that is—one acre for soldiers, twenty for colonels.

FIRST PEASANT: Well, well, well! So the rest of us, we not the army?

SECOND PEASANT: I wonder sometimes, Mr. Jupiter, when you start to dig around in that head of yours, where you does fish up such sharp-tooth talk. About the army and the rest of us—the army!

FIRST PEASANT: We are the army that suffers, Mr. Patience—
we are colonels, even, of an army of sufferers, and mark
my words, when we finally lose patience, friend Patience,
they go be hauled over the coals at the palace.

SECOND PEASANT: Well, well! As if you going there! Maybe you
right after all, comrade Jupiter: it have some things mashing up in this kingdom!

[*They go back to work, singing "Ago, Ago . . ."*]

ACT III

SCENE 1

[*The Royal Palace. The hall of receptions and festivals.*]

THE OLD MAN: Look, look! What a fine assembly! What a fine assembly! Nothing pleases me as much as to see all these black people from here with silk jackets and whole forests of plumes on their heads: blue, red, and white.

HUGONIN: Well said, old man, better to see them on our heads than on our asses, like our ancestors!

THE OLD MAN [*excited*]: Come forth, villifiers of our kind, of our morals, our character . . .

HUGONIN: Resign yourselves, it's his little fit of eloquence that seizes him every festival.
Quite so, old man, we'll hear you!

THE OLD MAN [*more and more excited*]: . . . and say that we are not worthy of liberty . . . and you, philanthropists of all nations, you strangers to prejudice, who recognize in us the stamp of our common maker, rejoice in beholding the objects of your favor respond so fully to your benevolent vision!

HUGONIN: Most excellent, old man! And I especially appreciate how patriotically the rum in you reasons and the clairin calls!

CHANLATTE: Don't get too excited. I have said all this once already, in more inspired language:

[*Declaiming, with glass in hand*]

> *Proud en'mies of our rights approved in war,*
> *Repent your errors, trouble us no more!*
> *Why should we care a fig for all your bile!*
> *How dare you think to trespass on our shore,*
> *Upon the mighty boulder of this isle?*
> *In vain 'gainst Neptune do the strong winds roar;*
> *At that god's glance, the sea is still once more.*

As for trouble and bile, tell me, Hugonin, you know everything, what news of Pétion?

HUGONIN: Of course, the future president Boyer is getting on well! So well that he hasn't promised not to make trouble along the borders.

CHANLATTE: Devil of a fellow. I ask about Pétion, he tells me about Boyer.

HUGONIN: You know Miss Joust, er, Joute, Pétion's mistress. Really, young Boyer is proving a formidable jouster. The way he keeps coming after her, he has boldly entered the tiltyard. And there, jousting hard and lustily, striking though giving no wound, but with a certain point, he's gotten the better of Pétion—who, losing his edge and tired of all this swordplay, looks like the Knight of the Woeful Countenance—get it?
> *He lost his shield, and now*
> *He cries just like a cow.*

[*A group enters, conversing.*]

TROU BONBON: By God, I'm used to these royal whims, but this one is really something! Is it true that the people, their necks stiff and their shoulders bruised from just building the Citadel, are now asked to make a patriotic gift by building, somewhere on the slopes of Crête-à-Pierrot, a new castle? And what a castle! A castle out of the Thousand-and-One Nights!

MAGNY: You should say the thousand-and-one days, but you know how one always exaggerates. We have only 365 days. It's written plainly in the *Gazette*. Look there and read: a palace for a symposium that would bring together all the world's sovereigns who will deign to push some little point as far as Haiti. In short, a timetable palace for an ecumenical conference!

VASTEY: My God, why not? With clouds and delirium over our heads, at our feet the hiccup of foam vomited up by two worlds, look where God has placed us! Our backs pushed against the Pacific, in front of us Europe and Africa; at our sides, either way, the Americas! At the confluence of all the tides of the world, at the node of all the ebb and flood, there is—at all points of this vista, the enormous spectacle—there is this extraordinary amalgam of the Atlantic!

MAGNY: My good admiral, you don't yet have any ships for your fleet, but don't worry: Haiti is itself a great ship, I would say more precisely a great galley,
and
The whole crew has tropical fever!

HUGONIN: Oarsmen, ready! Bit in mouth! The King!

[*Women pass by.*]

FIRST LADY: You are a beauty, my dear, that's for sure! A love of a dress, and your shawl has a really bewitching color!

SECOND LADY: Never mind that! Coming upstairs, I thought I'd die of fear! I get to the palace, I put my foot on the first step, and what do I see, practically breathing into my face? In plain daylight, a "frizzy"—one of those screech owls that bring you bad luck! I start running. I fall and get up again. And everyone copies me. A real panic. As if a guard had fired off a gun.

THIRD LADY: If I were you I'd say a prayer, always the same one, it always worked, you know, three times and really fast:
    Janman janman Ti Kitha pou'n goueh
    Janman janman Ti Kitha pou'n goueh
    Janman janman Ti Kitha

[*Silence.*]

A HERALD: The king!

[*The king and queen enter, preceded by African pages, clothed in their tribal costumes.*]

CHRISTOPHE [*to the assembly*]:
    Beloved and faithful ones,
    You are the great Haitian family
    And where would we rather be than in the bosom
    Of our family?

[*Laughter. Christophe strikes up Grétry's song, with choral response from all of the courtiers.*]

Where would we rather be
Where would we rather be
Than at home with family?
All is at peace
All is at peace
The heart the eyes
The heart the eyes
Live happily, live happily
As our forebears lived
As our forebears lived.

[*Laughter. Christophe presents the African pages to the courtiers.*]

Deliverance, Crown, Valentine, John. Well-beloved
orphans, torn from their mother's breasts,
yes, my good ladyfriend,
red, yellow, green,
the more cruel Fortune hardened herself
against them
the more I desired to clothe them
in the joyful colors of my favor
My Mandingos! My Congos!
I have ransomed them from the slave trader,
redeemed them out of the mire
and that all may know what delight I take in them
I have created a title that proclaims it well:
"The Royal Sweets."

A LADY: You have to admit that the Royal Sweets are adorable!

CHRISTOPHE: Charming ladies, don't upset yourselves. Know
that you too, each one more than all others, are our Royal
Sweets, the delights of my reign.

[*Enter General Guerrier, Duke of l'Avancé, and his wife.*]

Ah, just in time, here you are, our pretty Mrs. Guerrier. Prettier than ever—and surprised by her king while being unfaithful with her general of a husband! [*Laughing*] My dear Guerrier, to be rid of you, I need do no more than put you under close arrest in the Citadel.

GUERRIER: Your Majesty, I have no worry, my wife is virtuous, and you scarcely heavier than a current of air, so I may assure myself that the little Guerriers are indeed little Guerriers—to serve you and defend the crown!

CHRISTOPHE: A fine reply, my good duke! Good, we're not going to break up our friendship over a little pleasantry. Old friend, we still have so much—do we not?—to do together. I'll tell you, things are stirring around Saint-Marc. We must keep an eye on things there.

GUERRIER: They'd better not try it! There is a hand, and no weak one, ready to fall on them, Your Majesty.

CHRISTOPHE: Thank you, comrade, thank you! . . . And you, Vastey, Magny, my dear friends, what news? What do you talk of?

MAGNY: Oh, Vastey and I were just speaking . . . of the question of lands, Your Majesty!

CHRISTOPHE: What, what? . . . Do you mean there's a question of lands, and the king hasn't heard of it? How odd!

MAGNY: In my opinion, Your Majesty, the problem presents itself with a certain acuity, since Pétion's agents are spreading the news everywhere that he has decided to sell off public lands to certain private parties.

CHRISTOPHE: Oh, let him sell, let him sell!

And who will buy? The generals? The rich? The peasants? If it's the big shots, I pity the people! And if it's the peasants, I pity the country! I can already see the anarchy of the millet and sweet potato on their little parcels of land.

But enough stupidity! Besides, Magny, I find that for a general, you think too much . . . [*with a menacing air*] . . . I mean, way too much!

But here is our new archbishop, Monseigneur Juan de Dios!

[*New groups of invited guests enter. Among them is the new archbishop, Juan de Dios Gonzales, who approaches the king.*]

HUGONIN: Oh! I don't like this at all, not at all!

CHRISTOPHE: Hugonin, why are you sniveling like that?

HUGONIN: I'm saying I don't like seeing our monseigneur outmaneuvered by this monsignor. Look at him: when he arrived here, I took him for one of those scrawny wading birds—a *coulivicou*—with such a flat gut. Sure, all those Spanish chickpeas! But he's really a cormorant. Look at him now: plump, chubby, puffed up with importance and cherry preserves—he'll keep eating all the way to the ladies' hands!

A LADY: Don't speak ill of Monseigneur, Mr. Hugonin. If you had more religion and came more often to mass, you'd know what a fine bass voice he has.

JUAN DE DIOS GONZALES [*addressing* CHRISTOPHE]: Permit me to remind Your Majesty that in fifteen days, it will be the Feast of the Assumption. May I hope, along with the entire population of the Cape, that you will grace our ceremony with your royal presence, since it is one of the most important in the Roman church?

CHRISTOPHE: At the Cape? In this season, it's damn hot up there.

JUAN DE DIOS GONZALES: Your Majesty, this ceremony can be conducted with dignity only in a cathedral, and in the capital.

CHRISTOPHE: Oh. Well, you know, the cathedral is wherever you are, and the capital, wherever I am!

JUAN DE DIOS GONZALES: To be sure, Your Majesty. But only at the Cape will it have all the desired grandeur.

CHRISTOPHE: Juan de Dios, on the fifteenth of August, I will be in Limonade and nowhere else. If Our Lady wants to be celebrated, she will have to follow me there.

JUAN DE DIOS GONZALES: Your Majesty, allow me to insist . . .

HUGONIN [*interrupting him*]: Padre, Padre, por favor, do not insist! Caramba, is your head harder than a stone?
       If the Virgen de la Caridad loves us, let her follow us to Limonade! En espagnol Limonada . . . Comprende usted esta palabra?

SCENE 2

[*The Church at Limonade. Feast of the Assumption.*]

JUAN DE DIOS GONZALES [*officiating*]:
       Sancta Maria, ora pro nobis
       Sancta Maria genitrix, ora pro nobis
       Mater Christi
       Mater divinae gratiae

CHRISTOPHE:
> *Herzulie Freda Dahomey*
> *ora pro nobis.*

JUAN DE DIOS GONZALES:
> *Rosa mystica*
> *Turris Davidica*
> *Turris eburnea*

CHRISTOPHE [*groaning*]:
> Loko, Petro, Brisé-Pimba,
> all the gods of lightning and fire

JUAN DE DIOS GONZALES:
> *Regina Angelorum*
> *Regina Patriarcharum*
> *Regina Prophetarum*
> *Regina Apostolorum*

CHRISTOPHE:
> Zeïde Baderre Cordonozome!
> (Ah! She who stood on the mouths
> Of our cannons to point them straight—)
> *Ora pro nobis*

JUAN DE DIOS GONZALES:
> *Agnus Dei qui tollis peccata mundi*
>> *Parce nobis*
> *Agnus Dei qui tollis peccata mundi*
>> *Exaudi nos Domine*
> *Agnus Dei qui tollis peccata mundi*

CHRISTOPHE:
> *Miserere, miserere*

[*As if seeing a ghost*]

Woman, have no fear, for he
That braved St. Peter will have none
And scorns the cawing crow Corneille
Flying across his sun!

[*Threatening an invisible apparition*]

Saint Toussaint dead for our sins,
  Parce nobis,
St. Dessalines dead at the Red Bridge
  Like a god snared in a trap
You'd have said that the black fire of the earth was vomited
up through the frightful cleft
when he defied with his thunder the snares of five thousand
arms
  Miserere
  Miserere nobis

[*The ghost of Corneille Brelle appears in the back of the church.*]

JUAN DE DIOS GONZALES:
  *Oremus. Concede nos famulos tuos, Domine, mentis et corporis
  sanitate gaudere.*

CHRISTOPHE [*standing up and shouting at the priest*]: Juan de
  Dios, priest of the Roman Church, what sort of mass is this?

JUAN DE DIOS GONZALES: Corneille Brelle!

[*He falls.*]

CHRISTOPHE [*sinking down in his turn and groaning*]: By thunder! Who, who has set Bakulu Baka on me?

SCENE 3

[*In the sacristy of the Church of Limonade. Christophe is stretched flat, with his eyes closed, surrounded by the doctor and Christophe's entourage. Fragments of choral singing are heard from afar.*]

Heaven's queen
Break the chains
Of blackest hell,
Quench the vile
Fires below
And all their rage dispel.

STEWARD [*the doctor*]: Madame, he will recover, thanks to his unusually strong constitution, but it would be wrong to conceal from you that he will remain paralyzed for the rest of his life. You see, the overwork, the exhaustion, the nervous tension, and a great emotional strain as well . . .

CHRISTOPHE [*opening his eyes*]: Paralyzed . . . Steward, I see that I can count on neither your skill nor the science of medicine.

STEWARD: Your Majesty, we've done much already by preventing a fatal outcome. Thank heaven, you are now out of danger.

CHRISTOPHE: A fatal outcome . . . a fatal outcome . . . what a strange abuse of words. Is there any worse fate than that of a man, betrayed by that imbecile Nature, who yet lives? Who outlives his own powers? Steward, I'm not so stupid as to believe what my courtiers tell me. I am not king by the grace of God or the will of my people, only by the will and grace of my two fists. Oh! Better a good quick tap from the butcher. The poleax of Death. The beast cleanly flung down to oblivion. And you, and you, and you allow this fraud to happen. This assault of Fate! This attack of

Nature! Assassins! Assassins! Assassins' accomplices! See, you've let the future be assassinated!

CHOIR IN THE DISTANCE:
Star of the sea
Of the bitter spray
Calm the foaming wave
Drive death far off
Our trembling skiff
Guide home that we be saved.

CHRISTOPHE: Stop your canticles, in God's name, your songs of damnation. And as for the peasants who have seen a king collapse, advise them to muzzle their donkeys and gag their chickens. Woe to Limonade if I hear a single bray or a cluck!

STEWARD: Indeed His Majesty has need of calm and rest.

CHRISTOPHE: Not at all. Sirs, not at all. Approach.
I want to give you my instructions. Come now, approach.
What the hell, I'm not going to eat you! Look . . .

[*The ministers and courtiers draw closer to the bed.*]

Yes, my knees are broken, envious Fortune
has struck me down. But know that my soul
stands upright, inviolate, sound, just like our Citadel
Stricken, yet unshaken, the very image
of our Citadel, is Christophe!
So I shall continue.
You'll be the limbs that nature took from me.
I am the head, I have sworn to found a nation.
Is there any among you who will refuse to brace
its walls? To support its arches and vaults against hurricanes?
I expect it of you, I require it.

Sirs, with obedience as the chalk line
and work as the spirit level, the Realm continues,
Let it be known, its needful solidity roars
from our strength, across our marshlands
As for God
every man has rights, and every people! You gods, I do not
beg of you;
brandishing in your faces my people's scepter—
their staff with a hummingbird's beak in the side of a man-
of-war bird—
I demand for this people
its rights!
Its share of good fortune!

SCENE 4

[*Some weeks have passed. The Throne Room of the Royal Palace.*]

HUGONIN [*singing*]:
> *Damballah, he plant his corn,*
> *Yes, he plant his corn*
> *Mosquito bite him to the blood—*
> *This nation not so good,*
> *This nation not so good.*

CHRISTOPHE [*now old and infirm*]: My poor Hugonin, nations
are never good. And that's why kings shouldn't be too
nice either. By the way, Prézeau, as for the statue of the
Horseman on the Citadel, I have emphatically restated my
order to the garrison at Saint-Marc to transport the materials across the mountain—on their heads. Useless to wait
for what somebody calls the "right season." All seasons are
good if the king says they are.

RICHARD: Your Majesty, it's thirty leagues from Saint-Marc to the Cape. Saint-Marc is not in a very good mood, and the troops are exhausted.

CHRISTOPHE: Tell me—do you even dream of disobeying me? Exhausted . . . the soldiers exhausted. I am paralyzed, sir, but I am not exhausted. What's the matter with all of you? You would think a wind of sedition had passed through the kingdom.

RICHARD: Of sedition?

CHRISTOPHE: Yes, of sedition, Richard.

[RICHARD *withdraws.*]

SCENE 5

[*Officers come and go. Agitation and panic.*]

CHRISTOPHE: All right, what news do you bring?

FIRST COURIER: It's hardly good, Your Majesty.

CHRISTOPHE: I ask for the news and not your commentaries on the news! Prézeau, recall Richard. He can't have gone that far, and we're going to need him.

FIRST COURIER: The town of Saint-Marc, about to fall into the hands of our troops, made an appeal to the republic. General Boyer has arrived at Saint-Marc.

CHRISTOPHE: By thunder! I offered the olive branch to the people of Port-au-Prince! And they refuse it! For five years, Mirebalais has been a peaceful border. And they want to make it a bloody border! As it suits you. You say that

Boyer has entered Saint-Marc? And under the nose of my generals!

SECOND COURIER: Your Majesty, the generals Romain and Guerrier have gone over to the insurgents.

CHRISTOPHE: Romain! Guerrier! My generals! Swine! Horned serpents! These men whom I have covered with honors!
Take care, good sirs! Christophe is a big pit-stone
And he that would swallow a big stone had better be sure that his throat is wide enough! Prézeau, alert Magny that he is to take command.

HUGONIN: Caradeux, Your Majesty, is a fine plot of land outside Port-au-Prince, and if my information is correct, the senate of Port-au-Prince is making a gift of it to Magny. Magny has always loved land, Your Majesty.

CHRISTOPHE: Those shitty bastards! This whole country's a dungheap! How can Jehovah's nostrils not be offended by all this dung-water that steams in the sun?
Magny, Guerrier, Romain!
All right then, sirs, we can do without them, eh?
Moreover, we won't overrate their importance.
A few crampons that slacken; a few stones that come loose! But the arch of my wall is intact! Intact, do you hear me? Show Richard in.

THIRD COURIER: Your Majesty, at the Cape the people have risen up, and the mob has seized hold of the arsenal.

CHRISTOPHE: And the garrison? And Richard?

THIRD COURIER: The rioters have put out a rumor that Richard will not resist their actions.

CHRISTOPHE: Will you not finally bring Richard in?

[RICHARD *enters.*]

CHRISTOPHE: Sir, Count of the Bande du Nord, I wondered whether you'd come. But here you are! I flatter myself that you, perhaps, still fear me. The Cape is in revolt, it rises up. And you, the governor of that place, know nothing!

RICHARD: Your Majesty, one must consider that the situation is grave.

CHRISTOPHE: Consider . . . Consider . . . Disappear, you traitor! Get out! But before you go, villain, get on your knees and kiss the hands of your master.

[*Exit* RICHARD.]

SCENE 6

[*The Royal Palace, on the veranda. Christophe, ill, seated on an arm-chair. Beside him, a pair of binoculars, with which, from time to time, he scans the horizon.*]

HUGONIN:
> *One, two little branches,*
> *He puts his foot on the little one;*
> *Does the young boy know whose game he's playing—*
> *This is the capon-trapping game.*

> *The capon, the half-capon—*
> *But look, for there are twenty now;*
> *He retrieves his little stone*
> *In the conch-shell of his hand:*
> *Here come the birds to pinch him—Ow!*

CHRISTOPHE: What's the point of that idiotic song, Hugonin?

HUGONIN: I learned it long ago on the Dominican side. But King, I say only this, it took a strong back to stand the rinfofo

[*Singing*]

> *And rinfofo*
> *And rinfofo*
> *Drumstick cold, drumstick hot*
> *Dried-out meat and beans in a pot*

CHRISTOPHE: "Ambitious seeds," I said, "for our unpropitious lands," and raised my demands ten notches. Sweat proportional to the harvest. It was a cruel time. I regret nothing. I tried to put something into this ungrateful land.

HUGONIN: And look, from the land there are rising columns of smoke . . . In the wind, the whinnying of the horses. It is the royal fields burning.

CHRISTOPHE: I tried to make them hunger for action and demand perfection.

HUGONIN: Hunger, oh la la! You should see what they're gobbling down, how they bolt the king's ham and guzzle his wine; there's just one problem: their gross, rancid odor amid the king's perfumes.

CHRISTOPHE: Break! Break! Ruin! I reaped for them, only to reap the wind and their envy! Ruination and dust!

HUGONIN: The people live from day to day, Your Majesty.

CHRISTOPHE: I wanted to solve the enigma of this people that always drags itself down!

HUGONIN: The people go at their own pace, Your Majesty, their secret pace.

CHRISTOPHE: Stupidness! The others advanced by little steps over centuries. Where is our safety, if we do not make it ourselves—taking giant steps in a few short years, years full of effort?

HUGONIN: Listen, Your Majesty. Take this in, smell it. In the heights of the Cape, they're celebrating: the peasants cook in the open air, their cauldrons covered by banana leaves.

CHRISTOPHE: Your voice is strange, Hugonin; every word you say groans beneath the debris of my dreams.
    Because they had known abduction and spit, spit, spit in the face, I wanted to give them their place in the world so they'd learn to build their own dwelling, to teach them how to stand firm.

HUGONIN: And that beating sound, the beating of drums . . . Your soldiers will not stand firm, Your Majesty.
    The king's soldiers are beating the *mandoucouman*.

CHRISTOPHE [*listening attentively*]: By God, it's true. Those bastards! Those bastards! They're beating the *mandoucouman*.

AFRICAN PAGE: What does that mean, Your Majesty?

CHRISTOPHE: It means it is time for the old king to go and sleep.
    Not God, not the gods, nothing but night; the night that smells with its long thin muzzle; the maroon night of the bitter salt of winded blacks and the Dog.
    Night, you who accept no form and no scar
    among the abundance of nights, the unique Night
    I recognize, for you are the monkey fruit
    Of the great baobab of time;
    heart of the almond sprung free of the rigid seedpod of days
    Night of grasses and roots;

night of the source and the scorpion
I do not waver advancing toward our encounter
   But all this,
   Congo
is precisely said in a proverb of yours, of mine:

When you know the arrow is not going to miss you,
at least throw out your chest, that it may strike you right in your
heart!
Do you hear me: right in your heart!

SCENE 7

[*Dim light. The disturbing aura of a vodou ceremony.*]

MADAME CHRISTOPHE [*the queen, singing*]:
   My sickness lay me down, I cyan' get up,
   I going north, I'm not from over here
   God call me,
   I sick, I going to the North
   God call me, I going there [*twice*]
   I going north, I'm not from over here
   God call me, I going there.

CHRISTOPHE: Yet the forest, always young, puts forth its sap, forever sending it to the thinnest liana, the moss, the blue-fly, and the wavering firefly, impeccably giving each its due. And oh! Must this hurricane that chokes me, boiling in my heart, never again escape the contemptible confines of my chest!

   What a fine king this is! And who will obey him if his own limbs refuse him service?

   Congo, you have sometimes seen along your routes great trees, strong, inspiring awe, their trunks bristling upward with breastplate of thorns, though ruined at the bottom by a gash where the bark is stripped, oh! only the very bottom! They are solemn masts of a ship, ambushed by some cunning peasant, making their way toward their fall.

Oh, oh! They have ambushed me, Congo, just like that sablier tree peeled at the root!

[*Silence.*]

Caught.
Caught
In the entanglements of caught blood,
capsized sea-spume,
somnolent marsh, hoarded honey of my blood,
uproar I call you
call back to me
I once said: flight of fiery bees
I once said: great whinnying horse
of my blood.

[*Singing*]

Sun-O
Ati—Dan! Ibo Loko!
Sun-O
Legba Atibon
Ati—Dan Ibo Loko!

[*He moans.*]

MADAME CHRISTOPHE [*singing*]:
Sun, Sun-O, I'm not from over here
I am from Africa
Friends, where is the sun? Sun gone O!

Make a vévé for the lwa [*twice*]
Damballah mvèdo
Ago yo mvédo [*twice*]
Make a vévé for the lwa [*twice*]
Damballah mvédo

CHRISTOPHE:
   Gods of Africa!
      Lwa!
   Strong rope of the blood
   Father, fastener of blood
   Abobo
   Africa, my place of power
   Abobo.
   [*To the African page*] Congo, impetuous hummingbird in
   the throat of the datura, I have always marveled that a body
   so frail could hold without bursting the forward charge
   of my beating heart. Africa, sound my blood from your
   great horn! And let it unfurl to the full wingspread of an
   enormous bird!
   Do not break, cage of my breast!
   Beat drums, my pulse, beat,
   The toucan's beak breaks open the fruit of the raffia-palm
   I greet you toucan, great drummer!
   Cock, the night bleeds at the sundering ax of your cry
   I greet you, cock, with your deep-cleaving call!
   The kingfisher snatching up branch after branch of the
   oriflamme
   invents for itself a sun-drunken break of daylight
   I greet you kingfisher, great drummer!
   drummer-cock
   drummer-toucan
   drummer-kingfisher
   Drum! my audible blood.

Beat, great summoning drum of my heart
My initiates! My children! When I die
the great drum will sound no more.
Well then, let it beat, let it beat, let the great drum
beat me a river of blood
a hurricane of blood and life
My body!

[*He rises, takes a few steps, walks.*]

Papa Sosih Baderre
Thank you for my name of honor!
    [*In an upsurge of energy*] Hello, friends. My friends! Sound
the call for assembly. All of the troops! All of the troops!
My guards! My horsemen! Let my horse be saddled. Do
they think I can't fight? Bah! If Papa Christophe puts on
his tricorne on the heights of the Cape, everything will go
back to normal.

[*He appears on the balcony. Hurrahs of the troops. He rants at the
soldiers.*]

Soldiers
You know what sort we are dealing with:
miserable beggars!
What would they bring here but disorder, negligence,
laziness
Led by a coxcomb whose sole exploit
was to sprawl in the bed of Pétion.
We, we have built. They will destroy!
Did I say beggars? No, they are worms!
What lies in wait for you is a flabby, gluttonous
army of fly-by-night infantry.
They're termites, all of them termites, that's what they are.

Will you not defend the dwelling that shelters you,
your protecting tree,
your king
against this sorry army of termites?
Vastey will take command.

[*Speaking to Vastey*] Little mulatto, you're not black, you're mulatto. But just as the earth preserves in its foldings the trace of its past upheavals, you have known, . . . no, . . . you have *lived* in the red of your hair burning like fire, the infernal breath of the lightning; no? On your shoulders, there, between your two shoulders, I'm sure of it, the invisible collar, unbreakable; on the path through the sands, the caravan's sudden arrival: these are pains and horrors come from as far away as the underground caves; from these nauseous origins, yes? Ah! As deep as the rivers and our laughter also, that bursts forth like a red bull in the storm of the furious pastures of driven clouds! Therefore, you are black. In the name of disaster, in the name of my heart that raises my life into my throat with a belch of disgust, I baptize you; I name you; I anoint you black . . . well, then, little black man, do you feel the courage to march stir in your blood?

From Milot to the Cape, and then from the Cape to Saint-Marc!

Forward march!

[*He falls.*]

By thunder! Who, who? What enemy invisibly camped around my walls raises its powers against me?

[*The king's hallucination: Boyer appears, accompanied by his dazzling entourage of officers.*]

BOYER: The iron rod that he loved to brandish over your heads is at last going to break in his hands. Those who were once his officers abandon him, tired of being nothing more than his chief slaves. Soldiers, the vengeance awakened from within the heart of Providence sets forth to pursue him. Soldiers of the republic, you are also soldiers of God.

SOLDIERS: Hurrah! Hurrah! Hurrah!

[*The soldiers cross the stage to follow Boyer.* CHRISTOPHE *comes back to reality. The page helps him get up.*]

CHRISTOPHE: Africa! Help me to return, carry me like an aged child in your arms, and then unclothe me, wash me. Strip me of all my vestments, strip me bare—as when morning comes, one strips off the dreams of the night—of my nobles, my nobility, my scepter, my crown.

   And wash me! Wash me of their disguises, their kisses, my kingdom. The rest, I can do alone.

[*As he says this, he grasps the little revolver that hangs from his chain necklace.*]

SCENE 8

[*Enter Hugonin, in tailcoat and top hat, the distinctive formal dress of Baron Samedi, the death-god of the Haitians.*]

HUGONIN: Oh! This rum! I think I've had a bit too much. Real tiger-piss!

[*He clears his throat and sings.*]

Ogoun Badagry is a politic fella, oh!
Ah la la, he has cut the cord, cut oh!
Ogoun Badagry is a politic fella, oh!

I must apologize, ladies and gentlemen, for my little delay.

You know, I am always the one who arrives at the day's end,

And always in this shabby outfit of mine:

My tails, my top hat, I almost forgot my glosses . . . Oh! This rum! I meant to say glasses! But we arrive on time, and that's the important thing, for the moment of silence.

I say for the moment of silence, and of truth.

Attention, all of you! While soldiers hang some tuft of foliage on their shakos; while barons and dukes switch sides for their own advantage; while amid the ruins of their dances and the debris of their orchestras, the dancing master, embodying an outraged civilization, proclaims to all the winds of history that there's nothing to be done with these niggers; while . . .

[*He stands still and holds his hat in his hand as a shot rings out in the king's chamber, reverberating farther and farther.*]

Thank you! . . . The king is dead . . .
Bernard Juste Hugonin
Baron Samedi at your service!

[*He puts on his hat as he sings.*]

Ogoun Badagry is a politic fella, oh!
The master come or the master go
Ogoun Badagry, he always there

[*Night falls on the stage. When the moon rises, we are on the highest wall of the Citadel, the one known as "The Horseman."*]

SCENE 9

[*Echoes reverberate from vault to vault.*]

FIRST ECHO: The king is dead! . . .

SECOND ECHO: The king is dead! . . .

THIRD ECHO: The king is dead!

DISTANT DRUMMERS [*calling from hill to hill*]:
    The fire is out in the house
    The great fire in the great house
    The king is dead!

FIRST PORTER: Oof!
    Talk about heavy, you could say he heavy.

SECOND PORTER: Well sure, he a king,
    A king always heavy!

FIRST PORTER: Is not just that he heavy. I'd say he getting heavier.

SECOND PORTER: Maybe is 'cause he more and more king. You have to say it, he was a big tree.

FIRST PORTER: *Well big!* Have you noticed that all along, his body was pulling us toward this place? But now is just the opposite. His weight is his words, telling us something. We have to understand what he mean.

SECOND PORTER: Right—if he heavy, that mean he want us to stop. Whew! Let's put him down.

[They put down the body.]

VASTEY [*to the porters*]: Stand him upright.
　　In the ready mortar. Turned to the south.
　　That's good. Not lying down, but standing.
　　May he find, as he sinks through resistant gravel
　　and this stonework created by human hands, his own path.
　　And when he has found, alone, his true stature,
　　Let the moon, red tip of an arrow,
　　Hold up its terrifying torch!

MADAME CHRISTOPHE: And this country will have refused you
　　even the toad's pillow of moss,
　　And your country will have denied you the mud-cave of
　　the scarab
　　O man, extender of boundaries,
　　O man, forger of stars,
　　fierce, hot-clenching embrace,
　　great and devoted heart, already grown cold in the distance,
　　cast off your habit of stony pride
　　to dream of a small old woman
　　who limping through dust and rain in the broken day will
　　garner, at journey's end, your name!

AFRICAN PAGE:
　　Father, we place you in Ifé upon the hill of three palms
　　Father, we place you in Ifé amid the sixteen points of the
　　wind
　　At the double-faced blade
　　of origin!
　　Here, patience and haste
　　defeat and victory
　　Heap of shells dark against sunlight
　　exchange their spears, their tears.
　　Violence of night, flood-tide of day,

SHANGO
I salute you, O . . . when you pass
Through the hidden paths of the sky
Mounted on rams inflamed by the storm.

VASTEY [*addressing the king*]:
King, on our shoulders we have carried you here
by way of the mountain, at the height of the flood.
For your path had a name:
Thirst-of-the-Mountain.
And see, you are once more the king who stands,
suspending above the abyss your own memorial plaque.
You tender-hearted stars
you born from the funeral pyre of the Ethiopian Memnon
Birds that scatter the pollen
design for him his immortal coat-of-arms:
on an azure field, red phoenix crowned with gold.

[*Solemn fanfares and salvos of cannon.*]

Words from our translation appear in **boldface**. After a double virgule (//), the corresponding French appears in *italics,* followed by the page citation for the 1970 French edition. In cases where a French word or phrase appears in italics, we have so indicated by using ***boldface italics***.

We have also included Césaire's footnotes (so identified), as well as the annotations that he provided in a letter to Janheinz Jahn, January 27, 1964 (also so identified); these are cited as "AC to JJ, 1/27/64." We have omitted annotations provided to Jahn that concern typographical errors that were corrected or passages that were cut in the revision of 1970.

In glossing vodou terms, we have followed standard Haitian orthography except when reproducing the passage in Césaire's text, in which we retain his orthography.

3   **Archbishop of the Cape** // *archevêque du Cap* (8).
       That is, of the northern port city called Cap-Français in colo-
       nial Saint-Domingue, renamed Cap-Henry during Christophe's
       reign, and now known as Cap-Haïtien. It is often referred to sim-
       ply as "Le Cap."

5   **Don' ease up, Pétion!** // *Pétion, tiens bon!* (11).
       Kendel Hippolyte suggested rendering the creole pronunciation
       of "don't" as "doh," but we fear that this locution has been fatally
       captured by the gravitational field of Homer Simpson.
           In this prologue, the characters "are speaking in a very con-
       ventional French" (Jonassaint, email), though the cockfight is
       a setting in which classes and speech communities mingle. We
       weighed Jonaissant's observation against Régis Antoine's remark
       (Antoine 9):

> Kreyòl expressions abound; they are corrected in some way, or trans-
> lated into French, but in such a manner that the original language
> shows through. Thus, behind "Abrogat n'est pas mort . . . Insufflez-lui
> e l'aire," someone used to speaking Kr[e]yòl will hear "Abrogat pa
> mô . . . Ban'i on pè souf."

Accordingly, we have tried to bring out the creole inflections for an English-speaking audience.

It just ent natural // *C'est pas naturel* (11).
Kendel Hippolyte suggested "eh" to represent the Caribbean pronunciation of "ain't," but in the interests of intelligibility outside the Caribbean, we have rendered the word as "ent," following Derek Walcott's orthography. Allsopp spells the word as "en(t)," the parentheses indicating that the *t* is not always pronounced. Among the three pronunciations given by Allsopp is one in which the *n* is heard as a nasalization of the vowel with the *t* silent.

snake oil or chicken-hawk fat // *graisse de couleuvre ou de malfini* (12).
"malfini = small hawk (bird of prey). Its fat is used in the working of sorcery" (AC to JJ, 1/27/1964).

Take him out! // *abrogat!* (12).
"From the Spanish *abrogado*, removed, withdrawn, said of a cock taken out of combat" (Césaire's footnote).

Game-Master, pick up Pétion. // *Cariador, fais lever Pétion.* (12).
"Cariador = Spanish word, meaning the manager of the cocks" (AC to JJ, 1/27/1964).

6   **Pétion's a yard-fowl.** // *Pétion est un poulet savane.* (12).
Literally "savannah-chicken," glossed in Césaire's footnote as "a common chicken, inept at combat." "Cluck! Cluck! Cluck!" is our interpolation, added to emphasize the jeering tone of the speaker.

Rub his legs with some ginger. // *Faites-lui le cuir avec du gingembre.* (12).
"faire le cuir: Strengthen the skin by rubbing" (AC to JJ, 1/27/1964).

Kendel Hippolyte queried Yves Renard on our behalf about this passage and received the following explanation: "The legs of the fighting cocks are always plucked, and the skin is typically rubbed with something that serves to tan the skin and strengthen it, usually rum, or bay rum, or ginger. I think ginger is used because it also energising. So 'faites-lui le cuir' would refer to that process of making the skin leathery" (Renard, email).

O Mother, what a jook in the eyeball! // *Ma mère, quel coup de salière!* (13).
"*jook*: a jab or a poke; a wound caused by sth sharp" (Allsopp). Rhymes with "hook."

7   **"talented blacks"** // *"nègres à talents"* (15).
In prerevolutionary Saint-Domingue, this term referred to a slave with a specialized skill.

objective chance // *hasard objectif* (15).
The notion of "objective chance" (*le hasard objectif*) was developed by André Breton (1896–1966), founder of the surrealist movement and, from 1941 onward, a friend and literary ally of Césaire. In that year, Breton fled France to escape the Vichy government. En route to New York, his ship stopped in Fort-de-France, Martinique, where Breton happened to see a copy of the literary magazine *Tropiques* and was so impressed by Césaire's work that he sought out the author. One might consider this meeting as itself an example of "objective chance," since it was by chance that Breton's vessel stopped in Martinique and by chance that he stumbled on the copy of *Tropiques*.

In his surrealist trilogy (*Nadja, The Communicating Vessels, Mad Love*), written between 1928 and 1937, Breton understands "objective chance" as the accidental encounter of unconscious human desire with secret forces that prompt its realization in objective reality. Objective chance thus signifies the intrusion of the oneiric into the real, which blurs the line between subjective and objective reality. It reveals one's future as already written by past desire, so that desire and what proves to be destiny are brought together by chance.

Haiti arose from the smoking ashes of Saint-Domingue // *Haïti née sur les cendres fumantes de Saint-Domingue* (15).
Christophe's coat of arms bore the image of a phoenix, the mythical bird that is born from the ashes of its self-immolated father, and the inscription "Je renais de mes cendres" ("I arise from my ashes," or more literally, "I am reborn from my ashes").

12   **sugar candy** // *rapadou* (24).
"Unrefined cane sugar" (Césaire's footnote). Here, Césaire's gloss is not quite correct. According to Jonassaint, "*rapadou* is not 'unrefined cane sugar' but rather a 'hard brown sugar candy' (Freeman and Laguerre) shaped into roughly cylindrical pieces, enclosed in dry straw."

tobacco twists // *tabac en boulons* (24).
"Twisted leaves of tobacco" (Césaire's footnote).

long tobacco // *tabac en andouilles* (24).
"Leaves of local tobacco pressed into long pockets, [made from] dried peduncules from the trunks of palm trees" (Césaire's footnote).

aiguillettes // *tassau* (24).
"From the Spanish *tasajo*: meat cut into aiguillettes" (Césaire's footnote).
      The market woman calls out "*Tassau!*" twice; we have used the term "slices of meat" for the second iteration to set up an approximation of the sexual wordplay in Hugonin's reply "*Te donner l'assaut*" (which rhymes *l'assaut* with *tassau*). We render these words freely as **"It ent that meat I go slice!"** interpolating "coming after you like an army" to catch the military sense of *assaut*. Hugonin similarly puns on *rapadou* and *doudou* (sweetheart), and *akassan* and *agaçant* (in this context, provocative or exciting: "*L'agaçant, ce n'est pas ton akassan, c'est autre chose qui me remue le sang*" (24) (The thing that's exciting me isn't your corn mash, it's another thing that stirs my blood"). We have approximated this last riposte with an English pun: **"Forget about corn mash—I'll do my mashing with you!"**

Rude little devil! // *Mal élevé! Polisson!* (24); **Worthless scoundrel!** // *Vaurien! Goujat!* (24).
"These expressions are very French French" (Jonassaint, email). One reason for this may be that the market woman wants to signal Hugonin that she is not to be trifled with; for a succinct account of the social implications of Caribbean code-switching, see Alleyne, 168–71. We have adopted Jonassaint's suggestion for the first insult. The four French epithets are all nouns, but we have rendered them as two nouns modified by adjectives.

The second pair of insults is more serious, less bantering, than the first.

13   **Booboo!** // *Innocent?* (25).
In this context, the French word means a naïve person; we replace the question mark with an exclamation point, since the interrogative doesn't work in English.

That is the whale that tacks and veers . . . And he'll eat you down to the gristle! // *C'est la baleine qui court qui vire . . . Elle va vous manger un doigt!* (25).
This is a French nursery rhyme, *C'est la baleine qui tourne qui vire.* It belongs to the category of nursery rhymes about fish (*comptine des poissons*) to be mimed with fingers. Both words and music exist in different versions, but the overall meaning remains the same.

We have taken some liberties with the word-by-word sense in this song, in order to approximate the meter and rhyme of the original. A more literal translation of the last two lines would be "Beware of the whale / it will eat one of your fingers."

And if the back parts of Monsieur wish to be carbonadoed, same-same! // *Et si le derrière de Monsieur souhaite d'être taillé en carbonade, mêmement!* (25).
Carbonado as a verb is obsolete but persisted until the late nineteenth century (OED); it most notably appears in Shakespeare's *King Lear*, a play that Césaire acknowledged as an influence on this one (Laville 248): "Draw you rogue or ile so carbonado your shankes . . . " (act II, scene 2, line 36). "Same-same" is Anglophone creole for "the same" or "likewise."

As Césaire himself indicates in his gloss for Jahn, the French word is also antiquated: "Carbonade: Old French word = grilled meat/ beefsteak" (AC to JJ, 1/27/1964).

14   **Christophe, that's a man, he got balls.** // *Un homme, ça oui, et qui en a, le Christophe* (26).
In the French, "balls" is implied (by "en") but not said.

A Black man offers to pay reparations to those whom Blacks so rashly deprived of the privilege of owning Blacks! // *Un Noir pro-*

posant une indemnité à ceux que les Noirs ont imprudemment frustré du privilège de posséder des Noirs! (26–27).

This is the only use of *noir* as a substantive in this play. It appears frequently as an adjective, but for the noun designating a black person, Césaire elsewhere prefers *nègre*—which is with two exceptions in lowercase, in contrast to the capitalization of "Noir" in this passage.

I'll sell you my cow . . . My cow has been sold. // *Je te vends ma vache . . . Ma vache est vendue.* (27).

This song is adapted from a nursery rhyme. Césaire follows the original closely but omits the line in boldface;

> *Je te vends ma vache*
> *Bonne à beurre*
> *Bonne à lait*
> *Bonne à veau*
> ***Bonne à tout ce que tu voudras***
> *Un plat de morue*
> *Marché conclu*
> *Ma vache est vendue.*

We have used slant rather than exact rhyme in the last three lines, which allows us to retain the literal sense.

15 **pudding-stone** // *conglomérat* (29).
The French word *conglomérat* means more or less the same thing as its English cognate. In geology, "conglomerate" means "a composite rock made up of particles of various size." "Pudding-stone" is a synonym for "conglomerate" in this sense. We stress the geological meaning because of Christophe's obsessive construction of huge stone buildings, most notably the Citadel. The first part of the word "pudding-stone" also manages to evoke another central motif of the play, that of the preparation and consumption of food.

16 **THE MASTER OF CEREMONIES** // *LE MAITRE DE CÉRÉMONIES* (30)
"This is a white man sent by the TESCO (Technical, Educational, and Scientific Cooperation Organization) in order to provide technical assistance to underdeveloped regions" (Césaire's footnote).

17   **For a black king, a purple pageant, right?** // *Ce roi noir, un conte bleu, n'est-ce pas?* (31).
We have imitated the wordplay on the colors of the original; finding no suitable English idiom involving blue, we settled on "purple pageant."

Le Dictionnaire Littré defines *contes bleus* as "contes de fées et autres récits de ce genre, ainsi dits parce qu'ils étaient d'ordinaire couverts d'un papier bleu; et par extension, récits imaginaires, raisons sans fondement, billevesées" (stories of fairies and other tales of that kind, so-called because they usually had covers of blue paper; by extension, tall tales, baseless arguments, or frivolous talk).

So *conte bleu* can mean a fairy tale or tale of the fabulous, but also hollow or frivolous discourse, as in Molière's *Tartuffe* (1664), act II, scene 1:

MADAME PERNELLE:
Voilà les contes bleus qu'il vous faut pour vous plaire.
Ma bru, l'on est chez vous contrainte de se taire,
Car Madame à jaser tient le dé tout le jour.
Mais enfin je prétends discourir à mon tour.

Our translation:
These are the idle tales we must tell all day long
To please you, daughter-in-law. I try to hold my tongue,
But hours on end, you make the dice of gossip rattle
Until at last I take my turn at foolish prattle.

With our high-hat titles, Duke of Lemonade, Duke of Marmalade, Duke of Candy-Ditch, aren't we a sight! // *Avec les titres ronflants, duc de la Limonade, duc de la Marmelade, Comte de Trou Bonbon, nous avons bonne mine!* (31).
We have translated these place-names so that an English-speaking audience can understand the courtiers' fear that the titles will seem ridiculous to Europeans. As Vastey points out, there are French place names equally open to ridicule.

After all, the French have their Duke of Foix (foie gras, anyone?) // *Après tout les français ont bien le duc de Foix . . .* (32).
The pun on "Foix" and "foie" is untranslatable—"Duke of Liver" would not suggest the French place name "Foix." We have in-

terpolated the offer of foie gras to signal the pun to an English-speaking audience.

18   **Go stuff your precious esthete's fantasies!** // *Au diable, vos rêveries d'esthéticien gourmé!* (32).
Gourmé means stiff or pretentious, but it is also a homophone of "gourmet." We have rendered *au diable* as "go stuff" to call attention to this pun, which continues the play's motif of eating.

19   **His Magnificent Grace the Duke of Limonade . . . Mr. Lolo Jolicoeur** // *Sa Grandeur Monseigneur le duc de la Limonade . . . Monsieur Lolo Jolicoeur* (34–35).
We have anglicized the titles but left the French names as they appear in the original (*TRC* 34–35). Some, like "Limonade," "Marmelade," and "Trou Bonbon," ridiculed by the Second Courtier (see notes for p. 17), could be thought undignified, but many would not. We believe that translating these three titles sufficiently makes the point.

Césaire's list closely follows an allegedly "singular" historical document, dating back to 1819, that Paul Reboux received from "a Haitian friend" while he was visiting. The author's friend has not been identified; the author claimed to have copied sections from a book lent him by this mysterious acquaintance. What is striking here is the description of Christophe's court and its etiquette. Reboux uses the adjective *simiesque* (apelike); this word also appears in Césaire's stage directions for act I, scene 3. The historical accuracy of Reboux's source is unverifiable, but Césaire's play adheres to Reboux's order in the roll call of the nobility (Reboux 142). The roll call is, however, much longer in Reboux than in the play. Other names mentioned in Reboux (such as M. Rigolo,whose title is *Directeur du dépôt d'étalons au haras de pature de bronze*) appear later in the play.

20   **Madame Syringe, Madame Little-Hole, Madame Knocks-Out-Your-Eye!** // *Madame de la Seringue, Madame du Petit-Trou, Madame du Tap-a-l'œil!* (35).
In this case, we decided to translate the names, which strike us as selected for sexual suggestiveness.

21 **Well, claimed or unclaimed, we have to decide. And I say, "claimed." It's ourselves that we claim in our names! We, who were torn apart, must do the tearing.** // *Eh bien, griffus ou non griffus, tout est là! Je reponds "griffus." Nous devons être les "griffus." Non seulement les déchirés, mais aussi les **déchireurs*** (37; Césaire's emphasis). We have tried to be faithful to the sense of Césaire's highly compressed wordplay on *griffus* ("claimed, or seized," both as adjective and substantive) and *déchirés / déchireurs* ("the torn ones, the tearers"). Antoine (49) remarks that *griffu* also denotes a class of African animals that was emblematic of esoteric knowledge among the Bambara.

22 **Mere baby's rattles, no doubt, / But rattles are shaken!** // *Hochets, hochets, sans doute / Secousse aussi!* (38). Given Christophe's presentation of himself toward the end of the play as a quasi-religious leader (e.g., act 3, scene 7, p. 88), where he addresses his followers as *ounsi*, the initiates serving the *houngan* of a vodou worship community), one might connect these rattles with the sacred rattle (*ason*) "used to summon the [loa]," given to an houngan upon his initiation (Métraux 66). See also the following note.

A shaking, an earthquake, a white savannah / As my old Bambara ancestors said // *Secousse, secousse, savane blanche / comme disait mes ancêtres Bambaras* (38). "Secousse: This is a translation of a Bambara ritual. Cf. Zahan: Société d'Initiation Bambara p. 264. By this extremely elliptical phrase, the ritual represents the difficulty of manifesting [the] God's speech (Savane blanche = God).

"For this divine speech to be revealed, objects and the man himself must be shaken and moved, as one shakes a rattle to make it sound.

"For to understand the full sense of the God's speech, the man must bring about in himself a veritable interior revolution" (AC to JJ, 1/27/1964).

Profiterisne ... exhibeatur? (untranslated, 38-39; translated below).
CORNEILLE BRELLE: Dearly beloved, do you profess in Christ the Son and promise before God and his angels henceforth to

preserve law, justice, and peace, to make yourself subject to the Church and the people of God . . . and to assure vigilantly that due and canonical honor be shown to the priests of the Church of God? (*Pontificibus* could also mean "bishops.")

CHRISTOPHE: I [so] profess.

Barbara J. Newman, John Evans Professor of Latin at Northwestern University, has graciously provided these translations of this and the other Latin passages in the play. The Latin text of the first part of this oath (through "people of God") is recorded in an eyewitness account of Christophe's coronation by Julien Prévost, Count of Limonade (quoted in Leconte 263). The entire oath is a verbatim repetition of the one used at Napoleon's coronation, by Pius VII, on December 2, 1804 in Notre Dame de Paris (*Procès-verbal*, 44).

The stage directions found after Christophe's "*Profiteor*" (I [so] profess) are reminiscent of the famous painting of Napoleon's coronation made by Napoleon's official painter, Jacques-Louis David, in 1807—though in David's painting Napoleon is crowning himself.

A photo of Jean-Marie Serreau's staging of the coronation scene for the production in Venice in September 1964 appears in Laville (263).

24   *Shango, Madia Elloué* [*repeated*]
      Azango, Shango Madia Elloué [*repeated*]
      Sava Loué
      Sava Loué
      Azango, Shango Madia Elloué // (untranslated; 40).
      Shango is the Yoruban sky god, lord of thunder and lightning; he appears also in the New World vodou pantheon. The rest of the passage is in vodou *langage*, which is to say language that has a ceremonial rather than semantic meaning and is therefore untranslatable (Bailey 125–26 and note 38). In this and other instances of *langage*, we have retained Césaire's gallicized orthography.

25   **Plaisance, / places unpleasant to be in** // *Plaisance, / lieux où il n'était pas plaisant d'être* (42).
      We have tried to preserve the wordplay on Plaisance and *plaisant*.

Metellus's description of the hardships of the war is similar to that of the French soldier Moreau de Jonnès, who served in LeClerc's disastrous campaign to retake Saint-Domingue in 1802–3 (quoted in *TL*, 299–300).

26 **that was shared among all of us** // *tous entre soi* (43).
"<u>tous entre soi</u>: All (the blacks) gathered in a single family" (AC to JJ, 1/27/1964).

the imperious conch // *l'impèrieuse conque* (43).
"<u>impèrieuse conque</u>: In Haiti, the conch of a large mollusc called the lambi is used as a summoning trumpet. Here the conch calls man to combat. It gives the orders (hence the word 'imperious')" (AC to JJ, 1/27/1964).

Now, O Death, / I want to fall like a dream / in exile // *Maintenant ô Mort / je veux tomber comme un rêve / hors-parage!"* (43).
One of the definitions of *parage* in the *Littré* is "*espace de mer, étendue de côtes accessible à la navigation*" (a reach of sea, stretching along coasts accessible to shipping). So "*un rêve sans parage*" would be a dream that cannot make landfall. *Le Grand Robert* defines an archaic sense of the word as "*naissance, origine*" (birth or origin; compare with the English word *peerage*), and, in feudal law, as "*tenure de fief Indivis entre frères dont l'aîné seul faisait hommage au suzerain*" (joint tenure of a fief by brothers, of whom only the eldest pays homage to the sovereign).

All of these definitions converge on the sense of *parage* as some kind of definite and secure location, whether that of a ship in safe waters or a person enclosed by a system of kinship or sovereignty. We have translated *hors-parage* as "in exile," because Metellus's dream, once betrayed by Christophe and Pétion, can find no harbor, no kinship, and no territory, in Haiti or anywhere else on earth.

27 **harvests like none we've seen** // *des récoltes jamais vues* (44).
The French phrase could also mean "harvests [we have] never seen," but since Christophe is lamenting the destruction of rich agricultural land, we have construed it as harvests like none seen before, unprecedented in their bounty.

acacias // *bayahondes* (46).
"<u>Bayahonde</u>: Small thorny tree, called campêche in Martinique.
It grows wild and forms thickets" (AC to JJ, 1/27/1964).

28   **And you—may your eyes not teach you too late!** // *Et vous, puissent*
vos yeux ne pas instruire trop tard (46).
Antoine (23) says that "*ne pas instruire trop tard*" is an archaic
formulaic phrase; Magny is telling Christophe not to delay in
making a legal case ("*établir un dossier judiciaire*"). Despite our
admiration for Antoine's commentary, we fail to see how that
could be Magny's meaning in this context, so we have followed
the literal sense.

29   **upon to hear that which we are now hearing, I cannot refrain**
from sharing with this assembly something of the painful impres-
sion that I am suffering from. . . . What are you plotting behind
the back of the nation? // *à ouïr ce que nous venons d'entendre, je ne*
peux m'empêcher de faire part à l'Assemblée de la douleureuse impression
que je ressens. . . . Que machine-t-on derrière le dos de la nation? (47).
Antoine (32–33) notes the saturation of clichés in this parliamentary debate and, in this speech by the Leader of the Opposition, "howlers, or flagrant faults of enunciation: '*à ouïr ce que*
nous venons d'entendre,' '*impression que je ressens,*' '*derrière le dos de la*
nation'—faults that are not found exclusively among the orators
of newly-emancipated peoples."
The first of Antoine's "howlers" is flagrantly ungrammatical.
We have accordingly translated it ungrammatically, with a misuse
of the infinitive.

31   *A louse and a flea . . . You lousy for true!* // *Un poux une puce . . . tu*
n'es qu'un pouilleux (50).
More literally: A louse, a flea / on a stool, / who argued / while
playing cards. // The flea in anger / pulled out his hair / and
told him: My old fellow, / you're nothing but lousy.
This is a version of a well-known French nursery rhyme:
Un pou une puce sur un tabouret
Qui jouaient aux cartes, au jeu de piquet
Le pou a triché
La puce en colère passe par derrière

Et lui tire les ch'veux en disant "mon vieux"
Tu n'es qu'un pou vieux.

Some versions are more violent, including one in which the louse murders the flea and is "judged / By a spider / And imprisoned by a hedgehog / And hanged / By a turtle."

In our little workshop! // *Dans notre petit atelier!* (50) *Atelier* means workshop; also an artist's studio—and also, in prerevolutionary Saint-Domingue, a work-gang of slaves

32   ***This one plucks me . . . Lick the plate . . .*** // *Celui-là la plume . . . Lèche le plat* (52).
Again, this is a nursery rhyme, "*Une petite souris passait par là*," to be mimed, like "*C'est la baleine*," with fingers. Césaire uses the second half of the song:

> *Une petite souris passait par là*
> *Et sa queue traînait par ci*
> *Celui-là l'attrape*
> *Celui-là la plume*
> *Celui-là la fait cuire*
> *Celui-là mange tout*
> *Le petit n'a rien du tout*
> *Le petit n'a rien du tout*
> *Liche le plat mon petit*
> *Liche le plat.*

Here, our translation follows the sense of the original closely.

33   **How sweet the reeds upon these yell'wing plains . . . It rises, trembles, and o'erflows my glass.** // *Quels doux roseaux dans ces plaines jaunisssant . . . Monte, frémit, et s'échappe du verre* (54).
We have followed the original sense fairly closely, using the heroic couplet, the primary form of English neoclassical poetry. The apostrophes indicate elisions required by eighteenth-century English prosody, which did not permit anapestic substitutions in iambic meters.

Juste Chanlatte (1766–1828) studied in Paris at the prestigious preparatory school Collège Louis-le-Grand. Upon his return to Haiti, he became Emperor Jean-Jacques Dessalines's secretary and official poet. After the assassination of Dessalines in 1806, he served in the same capacity under Henri Christophe, who upon becoming king in 1811 made him Count of Rosier. After Christophe's death in 1820, he transferred his allegiance to President Boyer.

The song includes lines taken verbatim from "Epître à M. Desforges-Boucher, ancien gouverneur-général des îles de France et de Bourbon" (1778) by Ant[oi]ne de Bertin. In one edition of this poem, Bertin includes the following footnote regarding *roseaux* [reeds]: "Sugar canes. In addition to syrup and sugar, a very pleasant wine is also extracted, called, by the creoles, 'Frangourin' or 'Cane-wine'" (Bertin 66). Bertin, known as Chevalier Bertin, was a military officer and poet born in Reunion (previously known as the Isle of Bourbon) in 1752. He died in Saint-Domingue in 1790.

34   **part-time country priest** // *père-savane* (55).
"In Haitian speech, a casual, minimally qualified priest, a sexton who circulates through the countryside to say mass" (Césaire's footnote).

"Césaire's note is not correct. A 'pèsavan' does not say mass. . . . Freeman and Laguerre . . . give a good definition: 'unordained "bush-priest" who recites Roman Catholic litanies at Vodou services and at burial services' " (Jonassaint, email).

35   **Mane surgens Jacob . . . qui custodit eam.** // untranslated (55; translation below).
Jacob, rising early in the morning, set up a stone as a memorial and, pouring oil over it, vowed a vow to the Lord (based on Genesis 28:18–20). Unless the Lord build the house, they who build it have labored in vain. Unless the Lord guard the city, he who guards it watches in vain (Psalm 126:1).

Fit as a fiddle // *bon pied, bon œil* (56).
We have followed the usual translation of this French idiom, but more literally, it means "good foot, good eye"—it thus continues, as the English idiom does not, the horse metaphor introduced by Christophe.

What accents suddenly have charmed . . . saves his realm with touch of mantle royal. // *Quels accents tout à coup ont charmé . . . Qui sauve son pays touche au manteau royal* (56)

The first three lines are printed as if they were prose, though they obviously belong, by their rhyme and meter, with the lines that follow. We take this to be an error and have lineated the passage. Arranged thus, the poem has in all ten lines. Antoine (19) notes that all of the words in the first of these lines are borrowed and redistributed from one line in Racine's *Phèdre*, act 4, scene 5 (*"Quelle nouvelle a frappé mes oreilles"*) and two lines (17–18) of Lamartine's *Le Lac* (*"Tout à coup des accents inconnu à la terre / Du rivage charmé frappèrent les échos"*).

Césaire splices together excerpts from a much longer poem performed during the festivities for Christophe's coronation. The first six lines declaimed in the play appear in "Specimens of the Literature" (908). The Count of Limonade's record of the events, quoted in abridged form by Leconte, reproduces all ten of Césaire's lines, but piecemeal. Lines 7–10 are given first, followed by four lines that Césaire does not use; then lines 1–3 (set as prose by Césaire), followed by three lines not used in the play; and finally lines 4–6, followed by three lines not used in the play (Leconte 266–67).

36 **My noble friend Wilberforce! ... *We must give time due time.***
// Mon noble ami Wilberforce! . . . laissez du temps au temps (57–58).
Césaire uses both quotation marks and italics to mark the first quotation from Wilberforce, but only italics for the additional two.

Because we have found a source for virtually everything else represented in the play as a quotation, we intially assumed that Césaire is quoting from an actual letter, which he might have seen during his 1944 visit to Haiti or found reproduced in one of his sources. But we have been unable to find a letter containing the quoted phrases.

Some of the language here attributed to Wilberforce is already assigned to him in the first (1963) edition of the play, but in the earlier version, there is no mention of a letter. This may support the hypothesis that there in fact was no letter and that the revision invents one in order to give the King some stage business during his monologue.

We can at least report our negative findings. No such letter appears in the brief "Haytian Correspondence" section of the edition of letters edited by Wilberforce's sons (Wilberforce vol. 1, pp. 353–95). It is not in the catalog of Les Archives nationales d'Haïti or La Bibliotheque national de France. Inquiries to the British Library and the Wilberforce archives at the Bodleian Library, Oxford, and Duke University also yielded negative results. We did not find it in the histories of Haiti by Beaubrun Ardouin or Thomas Madiou.

37 **But not enough of black folks, Madame.** // *Mais pas assez aux nègres* (59).
Thanks to A. James Arnold for suggesting "black folks"; it catches Christophe's tone here.

38 **mombin tree** // *mombin* (60).
"mombin: scientific name spondias mombin. A large tree, native of the West Indies. The fruit consists of a large seed surrounded by a little acid pulp, and a thin orange-yellow skin, is greedily eaten by cattle and sometimes used for making jellies. In English: Hog-Plum" (AC to JJ, 1/27/1964; after "spondias mombin," Césaire's gloss is written in English).
We have retained "mombin," since the name is sometimes used by English speakers, and "hog-plum" has a decidedly unregal ring to it. Moreover, in the United States, "hog plum" refers not to *spondias mombin* but to a much smaller tree, the flatwoods plum, *prunella umbellata*.

39 **something to educate / rather than** *edify* **this people?** // *quelque chose qui éduque / non qui édifie ce peuple* (61; Césaire's emphasis).
In the context of the play, we take the primary sense of *édifier* as definition II, 1 in *Le Grand Robert*: "To bring (someone) to virtue, to piety, by example or by means of discourse." In the OED, sense 3b of "edify" is "to inform, instruct; to improve in a moral sense; sometimes ironical."
In both languages, however, the root sense of the word is architectural: to edify is to build. Given Christophe's passion for building, it is striking that he rejects this word in favor of "educate."

40 **cornerstone** // *pierre d'angle* (62).
"Pierre d'angle: architectural term, cornerstone. That is, the stone that sustains all the weight of the edifice" (AC to JJ, 1/27/1964).

sun's dwelling-place // *reposoir du soleil* (62).
This phrase could also be translated as "sun's rest-place," but the vodou sense of *reposoir* is "tree or any other place where a *l[w]a* is supposed to live" (Métraux 377). In a Catholic context, *reposoir* can also mean reliquary, which is perhaps relevant in light of Christophe's eventual entombment in the Citadel.

Right here! Rising! Watching! // *Le voici! Surgie! Vigie!* (63).
Césaire treats *surgie* as parallel to *vigie*, even though the first is a past participle, from the verb *surgir*, while the second is a noun. We have tried to convey the immediacy of this "verbing" of the noun by rendering both words as participles.

41   **Haïti is a big mouth** // *Haïti est une forte gueule* (65).
The metaphor evokes the topography of Haiti; compare it with the opening sentence of *TL*: "Let us imagine the mouth of an enormous gulf, with, to the south, a disproportionately projecting jaw" (Césaire 1981 [1960], 21).

42   **who are known here as "raft-keepers."** // *que l'on appelle ici des "radayeurs"* (66).
Radayeurs is not to be found in dictionaries of standard French; accordingly, we have translated it as "raft-keepers" rather than the more standard "raftsmen" or "rafters."

Aguay rooh-oh! // (not translated, 66).
"Aguay," or in Kreyòl orthography, "Agwe," is the vodou god of the waters, whom sailors invoke as their protector in times of danger. He is often addressed as "Agwé-taroyo" (Métraux, 102) or "Agwé-arroyo" (Deren, 82); the repeated cry of "rooh-oh" appears to be derived from the additional name. According to a popular belief, the Arbonite river is inhabited by Agwe.

43   **Mama Water** // *Maman d'Leau*
Maman d'Leau—more usually known as Maman Dio (derived from "Maman de l'eau") or Mami Wata—is one of several water-dwelling female *lwa*. She is usually thought of as both Rada and Petwo, capable of benign and malign influence (Houlberg, passim and 565–67).

44   **but not the climate, this time we living in** // *pas le temps, le temps que nous vivons* (73).
We have translated the first *temps* as "climate," the second as "time," in order to present both senses of the word.

45   **the stick** // *le cocomacaque* (74).
"Bludgeon, truncheon" (Césaire's footnote).

Bah! // *Hon!*
Le Grand Robert defines *hon* as "an interjection expressing discontent or anger, also surprise or admiration." See also note to page 67.

God is good. But far above us. // *Bon Dieu bon, mais haut* (75).
"'Bon Dieu' is simply 'God' in Haitian" (Jonassaint, email).

Métraux notes that while vodou practitioners also believe in the Christian God, this God "conjures up no precise image and He is too far away for there to be much point in addressing him" (83). "Too often the words 'God is good,' ending the account of some misfortune, have seemed the proof of the Haitian peasant's eternal optimism, when in fact they merely expressed his fatalism under the heel of a crushing destiny" (Métraux 84).

no way to worship the *lwa* // *pas moyen de faire un "petit service"* (75).
"Petit service: Ceremony honoring the African gods" (Césaire's footnote).

46   **"And so that my proclamation . . . *cannot exist without labor.* //** *En conséquence, voulant que ma proclamation . . . **ne peut subsister sans le travail.*** (76; Césaire's emphasis).
The language of this proclamation is identical, apart from a condensation of the first sentence in the last item, to that of passages in the preamble and articles 1, 2, and 13 of a decree issued by Toussaint Louverture, 20 vendémiaire an IX (October 12, 1800), quoted by Césaire himself in *TL*, 271–73. Christophe's "Loi sur la culture," although it is "directly descended from the earlier codes of Polverel, Toussaint, and Dessalines" (Cole 209), does not reproduce this language (Christophe 607–38). We note, however, that the Code Henry was published in 1812 and therefore does not include laws made after that date.

"Signed: Christophe." // *["]Signé: Christophe."*
"Agreed: Signed <u>Henry</u>" (AC to JJ, 1/27/1964).
This note responds to Jahn's suggestion in his letter of January 21: "'signé Christoph[e]': why not Henry?" (Thanks to A. James Arnold for this contextualization.) Evidently Césaire either changed his mind or forgot to make the correction when he prepared the 1970 edition.

47   **there'll be a Flag-Queen and a Singing-Queen** // *Il y aura la reine-drapeau et la reine-chanterelle* (78).
Among the offices held in the society of an *hounfò* are those of Flag-Queen (Métraux 72–73) and Singing-Queen (Métraux 71); Christophe is appropriating religious titles for state purposes.

48   **Contemplated instead the beautiful, the rare spectacle of a great force . . . but that it will crush us?** // *Comtemplaient le beau, le rare spectacle d'une grande force . . . qu'elle nous écrase* (79–80).
Compare this with the Haitian Noirist writer René Piquion: "Let us establish the mystique of authority. Force remains a beautiful thing, to be respected even when it crushes us" ("Force ou dictature," *La Releve* 13, March 1934; quoted in Nicholls 171).

49   ***Child of black Guinea born . . . languish as an unloved maid*** // *Enfant de la noire Guinée . . . Pour qui ne peut pas être aimé* (81–82).
Antoine (64) identifies this poem as the contribution of Ulrich Guttinger (1785–1866) to the "veritable fad of Ourika imitations, translations, and adaptations" (Miller 162) inspired by Claire de Duras's novel *Ourika* (1823). Since Christophe died in 1820, the inclusion of this song is a minor anachronism.
The poem was set to music (see Guttinger and Beauplan). For the full text of the poem, see Guttinger, *Mélanges poétiques* (1825), 123.
In the play, Césaire uses only the first eight lines and the last eight lines of Guttinger's poem.

51   **The little bastards!** // *Crécoquin!*
"<u>crécoquin</u>: This is an oath used at the time of Christophe's reign. In essence it means God-damned scoundrel! As one would say nowadays God-damned bastard, God-damned pig!" (AC to JJ, 1/27/1964).

It is a contracted form of *sacré coquin*; the *Littré* defines *coquin* as "someone of base and unscrupulous character"; *Le Grand Robert* as "a vile person, capable of reprehensible actions." We use the "The little bastards" (pl.) because Christophe's rage seems directed en masse at his backsliding subjects, "little" because directed especially at the children, whom he sees as unwilling to work toward their own future.

Tell Rigolo Socrate, for that's his name, that I'll stand for no rigmarole. // *Dites à Rigolo Socrate, puisqu'ainsi il se nomme, que je ne rigole pas du tout.* (84).
We approximate Christophe's wordplay on the name.

52 *The Emperor come to see the cuckoo* // *L'Empéré vini oué coucou* (85).
"vini oué coucou: this is in creole: come see the coucou" (AC to JJ, 1/27/1964).

Gustave d'Alaux (1816–1885) describes the alleged origin of Hugonin's song, which refers to Coucou Jonc, one of Jean-Jacques Dessalines's mistresses. This type of song (*la danse du carabinier*) was particularly prized by Dessalines to galvanize the military spirit; his soldiers would sing it while marching off to battle.

Dessalines's favorite mistress, Euphémie Daguille (also known as "mamzelle Phémie"), invented her own satirical variation of this popular song and dance. She added verses that ridiculed Dessalines's former mistresses. As d'Alaux informs us, the main "victim" of Daguille was Coucou Jonc, whose first name became the pretext of a version popularized throughout Haiti at that time, "Emperor, come see Coucou dance" (d'Alaux, 780).

Miming the double entendre of *coucou* (cuckoo/Coucou Jonc), one would dance to this air by jumping on one leg in a grotesque manner, either opening one's vest or agitating one's arms in the air as though they were wings. Dessalines himself liked this song and would add his own creative, highly demonstrative, and even grotesque, touches. D'Alaux describes Jacques first as falling on the ground, flat on his chest like a "rutting" elephant. Jean Fouchard notes that Christophe was shocked by Dessalines's demonstrative and grotesque dancing (Fouchard 84). As king, he banned performance of *la danse du carabinier*—hence his forceful interruption of Hugonin.

55   **good night, and plow hard!** // *bonsoir, et bêchez ferme!* (90).
More literally, "dig hard."

58   **mangoes** // *mangots* (94).
"<u>mangot</u>: That is, a wild mango (fruit, mangifera indica)" (AC to
JJ, 1/27/1964).

59   *One, two, three four . . . And for the king, the evil eye.* // *Un, deux,
trois, quatre . . . Pour le roi un maldioque* (95).
"<u>Maldioche</u>: Spanish (mal di occhio), bad fortune" (Césaire's
note). But *di occhio* is Italian, not Spanish.

    silk-cotton tree // *ceiba* (96).
"<u>ceiba</u>: large Antillean tree; very majestic, which resembles the
baobab of Africa. The scientific name is ceiba pentandra" (AC
to JJ, 1/27/1964).

    you're setting out on a dangerous path! // *c'est un chemin malouc
que vous prenez là!* (89)
<u>Malouc</u>: dangerous (Spanish: *maluco*) (Césaire's footnote).

60   **Who would awaken your stone of blackness?** / **To release, in its
striking, your human sound?** // *Qui réveillerait votre noire pierre, /
frappant clair votre son d'hommes?* (97).
"*frappant clair votre son d'hommes.* That is, the work that yields to
Man his true human sound. Work reveals the man to himself
and to the world, like a stick that strikes the drum" (AC to JJ,
1/27/1964).
    Compare this with Césaire's commentary on "A shaking . . ."
in the note for page 22.

    some burnt-necked niggers // *quelques nègres au cou pelé* (97).
One could also translate *cou pelé* as "bare-necked," but the other
sense, of the neck roughened by exposure to the elements,
seemed more central here. We have translated *nègres* as "niggers"
in this instance, because the king clearly intends it as an insult.

62   **agricultural tools** // *instruments aratoires* (99).
Instruments aratoires would usually mean tools for plowing, but
since the peasants have just been issued picks and shovels rather
than plows, the context requires us to broaden the term's meaning.

Nuncle // *n'oncle* (99).
"n'oncle : Popular way of saying uncle: (uncle) a familiar and affectionate term" (AC to JJ, 1/27/1964).
"Nuncle" not only stays close to the French, but recalls the fool's use of this term of address in Shakespeare's *King Lear*.
"In Haitian (creole), [one says] 'monnonk' (*mon noncle*)" (Jonassaint, email).

64   **Little ones, ol' ones . . . All them blacks in the mo'nes.** // *Petits ou vieux . . . Tout nèg' dans mo'nes* (102).
In the Caribbean, "morne" is the term for a large hill or small mountain.

hut // *cagna* (103).
"cagna: case, small house" (AC to JJ, 1/27/64).

This is a fine time to sing the leave-taking song. // *C'est bien le moment de chanter la Mazonne* (103).
"The Mazonne or Mazon: a song for taking leave" (Césaire's note). But Freeman and Laguerre define this word as a vodou dance or chant "to chase away unwelcome spirits."

65   **how a nigger of consequence works** // *comme travail un nègre conséquent* (103).
Conséquent usually means rational, responsible, consistent, principled. We have translated *nègre* as "nigger" to sharpen awareness of Christophe's irony: in the European discourse of the 1810s, the very idea of a rational, responsible, or authoritative black was an oxymoron. (See the introduction for further comment on the translation of this word.)
Our translation makes for a strong line in English but sacrifices the primary sense of *conséquent* and brings forth a secondary meaning. Yet the tone seems right.
Littré considers the use of *conséquent* to mean *considérable* (having authority, strength; that which needs to be reckoned with) to be a "barbarism," though he notes that the error is often made. *Le Grand Robert* admits this usage (definition 5), but cites *Littré*'s objection.
We intend a parallel to the British idiom "man of consequence," in which "consequence" has the sense of *OED*, definition 7: "Importance in rank and position, social distinction."

But we also hope to suggest the sense of definition 6, in which the phrase "of consequence" is glossed as "having issues or results, and therefore important"; the editors note a parallel to the French phrase "*une matière de consequence*," "a matter of importance, moment, or weight." Christophe is claiming, for himself and his race, the power to seize agency, to take actions that initiate historical change.

I don't like that tone! // *Je n'aime pas cette chanson-pointe!* (104).
"Chanson-pointe: satirical verse [of a song] that sets the tone for collective work" (Césaire's note; our interpolation in square brackets). This, according to Jonaissant, is another not-quite-accurate note. "[T]here is a satirical trend in a 'chanson-pointe,' but there is no link with collective work. Usually, it is a way of criticizing, [but] not overtly[,] an individual or a social or political situation. The chanson-pointe is a text to be decoded . . . , a conflicting [and/or] political message" (Jonassaint, email).

Twelve degrees per meter // *douze dégres par mètre* (104).
That is, with every meter (roughly 39.4 inches) traversed horizontally, the ground rises 36 centimeters (roughly 14.2 inches).

66   *Do not wash my head, Papa . . . When it's the rain that soaks it.* // *Ne me lave pas la tête, papa . . . Quand la pluie s'en charge* (105).
The song alludes to the *lavé-tet* ceremony in vodou, in which the head of an initiate is bathed in an herbal infusion "to establish a permanent link between the neophyte and a *l[w]a*" (Métraux 200).
   In addition to the clear reference to vodou, the expression *laver la tête à quelqu'un* means in French to reprimand someone very harshly (Leiner 103).

blows // *buffes* (105).
"buffe: blow" [coup] (AC to JJ, 1/27/64).

67   **Agonglo!** // (untranslated 106).
Agonglo was the eighth king of Dahomey (ruled 1789-1797); his royal emblem was the pineapple ("Kingdom of Dahomey").

Is Fate is God // so yé djé (107).
Jonassaint (email) doubts that this phrase is used in Haitian Kreyòl, but Nick André did not question it and approved our

translation. He confirmed our sense that its syntax, like that of our English, is ambiguous.

Peter, saint we all adore, / Do you challenge us to war? // *Saint-Pierre, Saint-Pierre, voudrais-tu / nous faire la guerre?* (107). By placing the line break after *tu* rather than *Pierre*, Césaire mutes the rhyme with *guerre*, we are not sure whether to regard this as a typesetting error or a deliberate choice. The lines appear the same way in the 1963 edition and in the serialized version (Césaire 1963; Césaire 1961–63).
Ivor Case remarks that "the St. Peter in question is not that of the Christian church. He is certainly the *lwa* St.-Pierre, who has the same characteristics as Shango" (Case 13). We propose that it may be both, given Christophe's double allegiance to, and transgressions against, vodou and Christianity within the play.

Woy! // *Hon!* (109). In its previous use (page 45; page 74 in the original), *Hon!* clearly expresses irritation, so we translated it as "Bah!" Here, it seems to express the two men's delighted surprise at encountering each other. We have translated it with the exclamation "Woy!," widely used in both Anglophone and Francophone territories of the Caribbean. Allsopp describes it as an "expression of great surprise, fright, or amusement." We note also its use, in Haiti, as an informal greeting. Freeman and Laguerre list "Hey!" and "Hi!" among possible translations.

69   **they go be hauled over the coals at the palace.** // *ils en auront pour leur grade au château* (111).
"*en avoir pour son grade, on en prendra pour son grade.* French expression that means <u>be well served, have one's abundant share</u> (of a disagreeable thing)" (AC to JJ, 1/27/1964).

71   **Proud en'mies of our rights approved in war . . . At that god's glance, the sea is still once more.** // *Et vous fiers ennemis de nos droits triomphants . . . Un regard de ce dieu rend la mer immobile* (116). These are the last seven lines of the "Chant inaugural" that Chanlatte declaimed at the coronation of Christophe (Chanlatte 244).

Miss Joust, er, Joute // *mademoiselle Joute* (117).
We have interpolated this self-correction in order to suggest the
wordplay on jousting and the name "Joute" in the original.

He lost his shield, and now / He cries just like a cow // Et perdant
sa rondache / Pleura comme une vache (117; Césaire's italics).
More literally: "And having lost his shield, / He wept like a cow."
Hugonin quotes directly from *Satyres XI* (Régnier 192 [204]) by
the French poet Mathurin Régnier (1573–1613). Césaire mod-
ernizes Régnier's orthography.

72 **hiccup of foam** // *hoquet d'écumes* (118).
Antoine (50) remarks that in Bambara tradition, the cryptic
speech of a god is evoked in the metaphor of the hiccup.

a great galley // *une grande galère* (118).
In *TL*, Césaire remarks that in a 1796 speech to the French
National Assembly, Admiral Villaret-Joyeuse "compared Saint-
Domingue to a galley, and, on the authority of this analogy, con-
signed its blacks to the fate of Roman convicts" (*TL* 248). For
certain offenses, the Code Henry sentenced perpetrators to the
galleys (Christophe, 517; 530; 575).

Oarsmen, ready! Bit in mouth! // *Alerte! Tap en bouche!* (118).
"The bit was a piece of cork that hung from a string around a
galley-slave's neck, which was pushed into his mouth before battle to prevent him from crying out" (Césaire's note).

73 **a "frizzy"** // *un frisé* (119).
The term names a "Hispaniolan barn owl, hoot owl . . . or
screech owl . . . sometimes considered to be a *lougarou* [female
werewolf] in disguise" (Freeman and Laguerre). Thus this sight
is doubly ominous: a night bird appears in broad daylight, and
it may well be a supernatural monster hidden in a bird's body.
(Thanks to Jean Jonassaint for drawing our attention to Freeman
and Laguerre's definition.)
　　We have translated *frisé* literally because it also suggests the
return of an Africanness ("frizzy" hair) repressed by the mimicry
of European courts.

Janman janman Ti Kitha pou'n goueh // (untranslated, 119).
This incantation is in *langage* and therefore not translatable.

Grétry's song // *le chanson de Grétry* (120).
André-Ernest-Modeste Grétry (1741–1813) composed this song as a vocal quartet for his opera *Lucile* (1769; libretto by J. F. Marmontel). "It was adopted by the Bourbons after the Restoration as a loyal air" (Grove 616). When the Emperor Napoleon arrived to attend the opera, it was played as he entered the theater (Barbier 125).

Césaire, given his studies of Hegelian dialectic in Paris and his former membership in the French Communist Party, might also have known that the first two lines of the song are used, with scathing irony, as the epigraph to chapter 7 of Marx and Engels's *Die Heilige Familie, oder, Kritik der Kritischen Kritik* (The Holy Family, or, Critique of Critical Critique) (152).

Another of Grétry's operas, *Zémire et Azor*, was performed at Cap-Henry (now Cap-Haïtien) as part of "the protracted celebrations of the queen's patronal festival on August 15, the Feast of the Assumption, in 1816" (Cole 224).

75   **Pétion's agents are spreading the news everywhere that he has decided to sell off public lands to certain private parties** // *D'autant que des agents de Pétion von partout colporter la nouvelle, qu'il a décidé de vendre aux particuliers les propriétés domaniales* (123).
Nicholls (54) notes that although Christophe passed a law on March 31, 1807, "providing for the sale of state land to the people," he delayed its implementation for ten years, citing "important circumstances." Shortly after the enactment of Christophe's law, similar legislation was adopted—and implemented—in the South, with the result that "[d]uring the presidency of Pétion [which ended with his death in 1818] over 150,000 hectares were distributed or sold to more than 10,000 persons."

76   **one of those scrawny wading birds—a** *coulivicou* // *un coulivicou* (123).
We have not translated the name because we are unable to determine precisely what bird *coulivicou* denotes. We have interpolated a description condensed from Césaire's note, "Bird, of the order of waders" and his fuller gloss for Jahn: "Coulivicou: (Martiniquan word): wading bird, gloomy and thin (very). In Martinique, one says thin as a coulivicou in speaking of a person who is very, very thin" (AC to JJ, 1/27/1964).

We found a reference to the *coulivicou* in the folktale of Yè as told by Lafcadio Hearn (Hearn, *Two Years*, 405–10). Hearn's note (409) says that:

> The *coulivicou*, or "Colin Vicou," is a Martinique [sic] bird with a long meagre body, and an enormous bill. It has a very tristful and taciturn expression. . . . [Hearn's ellipsis] *Maig conm yon coulivicou*, "thin as a *coulivicou*," is a popular reference for the appearance of anybody much reduced by sickness.

When we sought definitions other than those of Césaire and Hearn, however, we were stymied. Raphaël Confiant's *Dictionnaire créole martiniquais-français* defines *koulivikou* (the correct spelling in current Martiniquan orthography) as a snake (*couleuvre*). The word does not appear to be used in Haiti, or at least is not included in the Haitian dictionary of Freeman and Laguerre. There *is* a bird called a *coulicou*, and it is slender. But it is a cuckoo, not a wader. There seems to be some linguistic slippage between *coulicou* and *coulivicou*: three sources (Ballet 13, de Jonnès 432, Revert 512) use the name *coulivicou* to denote the mangrove cuckoo (*coucou manioc, cuculus seniculus Latham*). All three note the popular belief that the *coulivicou's* song predicts rain, but none cites the phrase "thin as a *coulivicou*."

We wonder if Hearn confused the two meanings of *coulivicou* (snake, cuckoo), and Césaire—who acknowledged Hearn as one of his sources for Martiniquan folklore (Ménil and Césaire)—followed suit. How the mangrove cuckoo became a wading bird is beyond our conjecture.

77 (**The Latin liturgy) Sancta Maria, ora pro nobis . . . sanitate gaudere** // (untranslated, 125–27; translated below).

Holy Mary, pray for us.
Holy Mother of God, pray for us.
Mother of Christ . . .
Mother of divine grace . . .
Mystical rose . . .
Tower of David . . .
Tower of ivory . . .
Queen of angels . . .
Queen of patriarchs . . .
Queen of prophets . . .
Queen of apostles . . . pray for us.

Agnus Dei
Lamb of God, who takest away the sins of the world, spare us.
Lamb of God, who takest away the sins of the world, hear us, O Lord.
Lamb of God, who takest away the sins of the world, have mercy, have
mercy.
Prayer
Let us pray. Grant us thy servants, O Lord, to enjoy perpetual health
of mind and body.
The first eleven lines are from the Litany for the Virgin Mary.

78   **Herzulie Freda Dahomey** // (untranslated, 126).
A female *lwa* whose domain of influence is love.

Loko, Petro, Brisé-Pimba // (untranslated, 126).
Loko is a "spirit of vegetation and guardian of sanctuaries" (Métraux 396), though he can also be a warrior god (Leiner 101).
       Petwo (to use the current standard orthography) can refer to
an entire branch of the vodou pantheon but more specifically,
as here, to the violent *lwa* Dan Petwo—or, per Métraux (84),
Dompèdre.
       Métraux describes a worshipper possessed by Brisé as becom-
ing "a hard and furious god" (235); as Brisé-Pimba, he is among
the *lwa* cited by Joan Dayan (35) as especially associated with the
Haitian Revolution.

Zeïde Baderre Cordonozome // (untranslated, 126).
The guardian *lwa* of artillery (Leiner 101).

79   **Woman, have no fear, for he . . . Flying across his sun!** // *Femme,*
n'aie peur . . . volant dans son soleil! (127).
The archbishop's given name, Corneille, means "crow" in French.

St. Dessalines dead at the Red Bridge // *Saint Dessalines mort au*
Pont Rouge (127).
On October 17, 1806, as he was marching to put down a rebel-
lion in the South, Emperor Dessalines was ambushed and killed
at Pont-Rouge, a plantation near Port-au-Prince (Leconte 189,
Cole 150–53), so called because of its bridge with red handrails
(Cole 151).

Bakulu Baka // (untranslated, 128).
"Bakulu Baka: a malevolent deity of the Petwo rite" (Césaire's note). Petwo is the more violent branch of vodou, Rada the more benign. Anthropological descriptions of Bakulu Baka do not quite agree with Césaire's note. A Baka is an "evil spirit" (Métraux 374) but not itself a *lwa*. It may serve a *lwa* or a vodou adept in exacting vengeance; it may also gain power over the person who has summoned it (Métraux 289).

80   *Heaven's queen . . . And all their rage dispel. // Reine des cieux . . . Et sauve nous de sa rage* (128).
From the canticle "The Hymn of St. Casimir," which opens with "*Reine des cieux.*" Of the six lines taken from the fourth stanza of the hymn, Césaire omits an important one: "*Les fers de son esclavage.*" The omitted line specifies the chains (*fers*) as those of slavery, though in the hymn, slavery is understood metaphorically as the bondage of sin:

> *Des noirs enfers*
> *Brise les fers,*
> **Les fers de son esclavage;**
> *Eteins les feux*
> *De l'antre affreux*
> *Et sauve-nous de sa rage.*

81   *Star of the sea . . . Guide home that we be saved. // Astre des mers . . . Notre nacelle tremblant* (130).
From the fifth stanza of "The Hymn of St. Casimir." "Star of the sea" is a common epithet for the Virgin Mary, playing on the closeness of *mare*, the Latin word for "sea," to her name.

82   **their staff with a hummingbird's beak in the side of a man-of-war bird //** *sa récade bec de colibri dans le flanc du milan* (131).
Colibri (the name means "hummingbird") is a hero in Martiniquan folklore. Despite his diminutive size, he vanquishes all comers until his defeat by the armored fish (*poisson armé*). See Hearn, "Conte Colibri."

Damballah, he plant his corn . . . This nation not so good. */ / Damballah planté maïs li . . . Ah! la nation pas bon!* (132).

"bête piqué sang li: In creole: the bug (mosquito) has pricked his skin and drawn blood" (AC to JJ, 1/27/1964). Damballah, one of the most powerful among the *lwa*, is the creator of life. Jonaissant (email) notes that *bon* has the moral sense of good, rather than the physiological sense of well or healthy, in this passage.

85   ***One, two little branches . . . Here come the birds to pinch him—Ow!*** */ / Une, deux petites branches. . . . Voici que vient le pinçon* (137).

86   **rinfofo** */ /* (untranslated, 137).
"chapon rinfofo: These are the inane words of a (black) Brazilian popular song: chapon = chicken; rinfofo: this is an onomotopoeia" (AC to JJ, 1/27/1964). In the 1970 revision, *chapon* has been dropped, though it appears in Hugonin's previous song (page 133), where we have translated it as "capon."

and raised my demands ten notches */ / et haussé de dix coches le niveau exigé de l'étiage* (137–38).
"[T]en notches: (coche = notch)
"The notch is the mark by which one marks the height of the water during a flood; here, the height of the effort to accomplish" (AC to JJ, 1/27/1964).

87   **The king's soldiers are beating the *mandoucouman.*** */ / Les soldats du roi battent le mandoucouman* (139).
"[M]andoucouman: i.e., the drumbeat that, in the Haitian army, gives the signal to retreat. In French, it would be the chamade (more or less)" (AC to JJ, 1/27/1964).

88   **night of the source and the scorpion** */ / nuit des sources et du scorpion* (140).
The French word *source* can either mean "source" (origin) or "freshet" (spring). Because the English word "springs" evokes coils of metal rather than freshets, and the English plural "sources" usually refers to the origin of information rather than water, we have used the singular form, "source."

My sickness lay me down, I cyan' get up . . . God call me, I going there.
/ / Moin malad m-couche m-pa se levé . . . Bon dié rélé-m, m-pralé! (141).
Thanks to Nick André for slightly amending our translation of
this song.
Cyan in Anglophone Caribbean creole means "can't."

89   *Sun-O . . . Ati—Dan Ibo Loko! //* (untranslated, 142).
Apart from the names of the *lwa*, this song is in *langage*.

Sun, Sun-O, I'm not from over here . . . Damballah mvédo // Solé,
Solé-ô, moin pa moun icit . . . Damballah mvédo (142–43).
Lines 5, 6, and 8 of this song are in *langage*. Again, our thanks to
Nick André for his help.

90   **Abobo //** (untranslated, 143).
"Ritual acclamation which punctuates the end of rada songs. Ut-
tered, too, during ceremonies as a sign of personal satisfaction.
The exclamation is sometimes accompanied by the noise produced by striking the mouth with the fingers" (Métraux 373).

91   **My initiates!** *// Mes hounsis!* (144).
In a vodou *hounfô*, the *ounsi* are officers of the temple, assisting
the *houngan*; they are not priests but they have been initiated
into the mysteries (Métraux 69–73).

Papa Sosih Baderre // (untranslated, 144).
The *lwa* of the winds (Leiner 101).

92   **and our laughter also, that bursts forth like a red bull in the
storm of the furious pastures of driven clouds!** *// et notre rire
aussi comme le taureau rouge jaillissant pendant l'orage du forcené pâtis
des nuages remués!* (146).
"[E]t notre rire etc. . . . That is, the laughter of blacks compared
with the thunder in the sky heavy with clouds. In so-called primitive poetry thunder is compared to a bull that tears up the pasture. Thus, laughter of blacks is compared to thunder; and the
thunder itself, compared to a bull" (AC to JJ, 1/27/64).

93   **Baron Samedi //** (untranslated, 147).
Baron Samedi is one of the family of *gedé, lwa* associated with
death and with cemeteries. His characteristic attire and pen-

chant for obscene punning are described in Métraux (112–13 and passim). Métraux notes that "even the most powerful sorcerer cannot kill a man if Baron [Samedi] has not first marked out his grave" (267). Christophe believes that he is the victim of sorcery ("Who, who has set Bakula Baku on me?," page 79). One might infer that in this speech, the Baron authorizes the death that immediately follows, speaking through Hugonin as the *lwa* do while possessing their human worshippers. Yet the scene also observes a convention of ancient Greek tragedy, in that the death of the protagonist occurs offstage and is announced to the audience by a messenger.

Real tiger-piss! // *du vrai pissat de tigre* (148).
See note below on "I almost forgot my glosses . . ."

94   *Ogoun Badagry is a politic fella, oh!* . . . *Ogoun Badagry is a politic fella, oh!* // *Ogoun Badagry c'est Neg politique oh!* . . . *Ogoun Badagry c'est Neg politique oh!* (148).
Freeman and Laguerre define the Kreyòl word *nèg* (a cognate of the French *nègre*) as "man, male; Black man; friend, pal, guy, fellow . . ."

The first, repeated line of this song also appears in the song "Ogou Balendyo *nèg politik*" ("Ogou[n] Badagr[y], political fellow"), included in Alan Lomax's *Recordings in Haiti* (CD 10, track 6). The annotator and translator, Gage Averill, remarks that "by politik, the lyrics don't suggest that Ogou Badagri is concerned with the politics of the state, but rather with relations, proper procedure, etiquette and protocol" (liner notes, 145). We have therefore translated *politique* as "politic" rather than "political."

Métraux (107) notes that "Og[o]u[n] Badagr[y] (of the great family of Nago *l[w]a* delights in the din of battle and probably that is why a vodo[u] hymn makes him the master of lightning and storm, a role which by Nago tradition devolves upon Shango, a *l[w]a* of the same group."

Césaire opens the song with a quotation mark but does not close the quotation; we take this to be an error.

I almost forgot my glosses ... Oh! This rum! I meant to say glasses! // *J'allais oublier mes doubles languettes ... Oh! ce rhum!* ... *je ve`ux dire mes lunettes* (148).

Here and above ("Real tiger-piss!") Césaire closely follows Métraux's examples of the obscene punning of the *gede*. "Lunettes (spectacles), in their mouth become *doubles languettes* (double clitoris), rum becomes *pissetigue* ..." (113). The definition of *languette* as "clitoris" does not appear in the *Dictionnaire Littré* or *Le Grand Robert*; the literal meaning is "little tongue," hence the relation to speech signalled in our choice of "glosses."

96 **ready mortar** // *mortier gâché* (151).

In other contexts, *gâché* can mean "wasted" or "spoiled"—this second meaning invites the reflection that Christophe's grandiose building projects have been a tragic waste of energies that might have been better directed elsewhere.

Father, we place you in Ifé // *Père, nous t'installons à Ifé* (152).

"Ifé" names both a city of medieval Africa and, in the diaspora, a mythical destination of the dead to which they are returned to Africa. African sources depict Ifé as set on a hilltop, but in the New World it has often been imagined to lie at the bottom of the sea, as in the "voyage to Ifé" ceremony in honor of Agwé (Case 22, Antoine 97).

At the double-faced blade / of origin! // *A l'origine / biface!* (152).
The *biface* is a primitive double-edged blade, made of stone.

97 **on an azure field, red phoenix crowned with gold** // *d'azur au Phénix de gueules coronné d'or*
As noted in our introduction, these words are taken from an edict of 1811 "announcing, in the terms of heraldry, the arms of the king" (Harris, *L'humanisme*, 119).

WORKS CITED

Alleyne, Mervyn C. "The Caribbean as a Language Area." In *Caribbean Contours*, ed. Sidney W. Mintz and Sally B. Price, 155–79. Baltimore: Johns Hopkins University Press, 1985.

Allsopp, Richard, ed. *Dictionary of Caribbean English Usage; with a French and Spanish supplement edited by Jeannette Allsopp*. Oxford: Oxford University Press, 1996.

Antoine, Régis. *La tragédie du roi Christophe de Aimé Césaire*. Paris: Bordas, 1984.

Arnold, A[lbert] James. "Césaire and Shakespeare: Two Tempests." *Comparative Literature* 30, no. 3 (Summer 1978).

———, coordinateur. *Aimé Césaire: Poésie, théâtre, essais et discours: Édition critique*. France: Planète Libre/Éditions CNRS, 2013.

Arnold, A[lbert] James, and Clayton Eshleman, trans. and ed. *Aimé Césaire: Solar Throat Slashed: The Unexpurgated 1948 Edition*. Middletown, Conn.: Wesleyan University Press, 2011.

Attoun, Lucien. "Aimé Césaire et le théâtre nègre." In *Le Théâtre*, 96–116. Paris: Christian Bourgois, 1970/1971.

Bailey, Marianne Wichmann. *The Ritual Theatre of Aimé Césaire*. Tübingen: Gunter Narr Verlag, 1992.

Ballet, Jules. *La Guadeloupe: Renseignements sur l'histoire, la flore, la faune, la géologie, la minéralogie, l'agriculture, le commerce, l'industrie, l'administration*. Volumes 1–2: 1625–1715. Basse-terre, Guadeloupe: Government Printery, 1894. Available at books.google.com; accessed January 27, 2014.

Barbier, Patrick. *Opera in Paris 1800–1850*. Portland, Ore.: Amadeus Press, 1995. (Translation by Robert Luoma of Barbier's *La vie quotidienne à L'Opera au temps de Rossini et de Balzac: Paris 1800–1850*. Paris: Hachette, 1987.)

Bradby, David. *Modern French Drama: 1940–1990*. Cambridge, UK.: Cambridge University Press, 1991.

Breslin, Paul. "Intertextuality, Translation, and Postcolonial Misrecognition in Aimé Césaire." In *Analyzing World Fiction: New Horizons in Narrative Theory*, edited by Frederick Luis Aldama, 245–67. Austin: University of Texas Press, 2011.

Breton, André. *Nadja*. Paris: Gallimard, 1963.

Case, Ivor. "Şhango oba ko so: les vodoun dans la tragédie du roi Chris-tophe." *Cahier Césairiens* 2 (1975): 9–24.

Césaire, Aimé. *Et les chiens se taisaient,* manuscript version, 1943, ed. Alex Gil. Archive of Yvan and Claire Goll, St. Dié, France. Our thanks to Professor Gil for providing his edited transcription of this document.

———. Aimé Césaire to Jahnheinz Jahn, 27 January 1964. Archive, Institut für Asien- und Afrikawissenschaften.

———. *La tragédie du Roi Christophe,* act 1. *Présence Africaine* 4 (1961): 125–55.

———. *La tragédie du Roi Christophe,* act 2. *Présence Africaine* 4 (1962): 146–65.

———. *La tragédie du Roi Christophe,* act 3. *Présence Africaine* 2 (1963): 163–85.

———. *La tragédie du Roi Christophe* (complete play). Paris: Présence Africaine, 1963.

———. *La tragédie du Roi Christophe* (completely revised by the author). Paris : Présence Africaine, 1970.

———. *Toussaint Louverture: La révolution français et le problème colonial.* Paris: Présence Africaine, 1981 [1960].

Chanlatte, Juste. "Chant inaugural, par M. Juste Chanlade [sic], Comte de Rosier, pour le couronnement du roi d'Haïty [sic]." *L'Esprit des journaux, français et étrangers* 9. Société des gens de lettres. Reprint of article of September 1814: 241–44. Available at books.google.be /books; accessed January 27, 2014.

Christophe, Henri (King Henry I). *Code Henry: Cap-Henry, P. Roux, imprimeur du Roi, 1812.* Available at www.archive.org/details/codehen ry00hait; accessed January 27, 2014.

Cole, Hubert. *Christophe, King of Haiti.* New York: Viking, 1967.

Confiant, Raphaël. *Aimé Césaire: Une traversée paradoxale du siècle.* Paris: Éditions Stock, 1993.

———. *Dictionnaire créole martiniquais-français.* Matoury, Guyane: Ibis rouge éditions, 2007.

D'Alaux, Gustave. "Les Moeurs et la littérature nègres." *La Revue des deux mondes* 14 (1852). Available at books.google.com; accessed August 20, 2012.

Davis, Gregson. *Aimé Césaire.* Cambridge: Cambridge University Press, 1997.

Dayan, Joan. *Haiti, History, and the Gods.* Berkeley: University of California Press, 1998.

De Bertin, Antoine. "Épître à M. Desforges-Boucher, ancien gouverneur-général des îles de France et de Bourbon" (1778). In de Bertin, *Oeuvres de Bertin*, vol. 2, 57–71. Paris: Froment, 1823. Available at books .google.com.

De Jonnès, André Moreau. *Histoire physique des Antilles Françaises: Savoir: Martinique et les îsles de la Guadeloupe.* Paris: Migneret Printery, 1822. Available at books.google.com; accessed January 27, 2014.

Dubois, Laurent. *Avengers of the New World: The Story of the Haitian Revolution.* Cambridge, Mass.: The Belknap Press of Harvard University, 2004.

Eshleman, Clayton, and Annette Smith, trans. *Aimé Césaire: The Collected Poems.* Berkeley: University of California Press, 1983.

Fenton, Louise. "Pétion, Alexandre Sabès (1770–1818)." In *Encyclopedia of Slave Resistance and Rebellion*, vol. 2, ed. Junius P. Rodriguez, 375–76. Westport, Conn.: Greenwood Press, 2007.

Fonkoua, Romuald. *Aimé Césaire (1913–2008).* Paris: Perrin, 2010.

Freeman, Bryant C., and Jowel C. Laguerre. *Haitian-English Dictionary.* Lawrence, Kans.: Institute of Haitian Studies, University of Kansas, 1996.

Geggus, David Patrick. *Haitian Revolutionary Studies.* Bloomington, Ind.: Indiana University Press, 2002.

Gil, Alex. "Migrant Textuality: On the Fields of Aimé Césaire's *Et les chiens se taisaient.*" Dissertation, University of Virginia, 2012.

Griggs, Earl Leslie, and Clifford H. Prater, eds. *Henry Christophe and Thomas Clarkson: A Correspondence.* Berkeley: University of California Press, 1952.

Grove, Sir Charles. "Où peut-on être mieux q'au sein de sa famille?" In *Grove's Dictionary of Music and Musicians*, vol. 3. London: Macmillan, 1900. Available at books.google.com; accessed January 27, 2014.

Guttinguer, Ulric. *Mélanges poétiques*, 2nd ed. Paris: Lebel, 1825. (In French sources, "Guttinger" is spelled "Guttinguer.") Available at books.google.com; accessed January 27, 2014.

Guttinger, Ulric, and M. Amédée de Beauplan. *Ourika: Romance.* Lyrics by Guttinger; adapted for music by Beauplan. Available at books .google.com; accessed January 27, 2014.

Harris, Rodney E[lton]. "The English Translations of Césaire's Theatre." *Cahiers Césairien* 1 (Spring 1974): 32–34.

———. *L'humanisme dans le théâtre d'Aimé Césaire.* Sherbrooke, Québec, Canada: Editions Naaman, 1973.

Hearn, Lafcadio. "Conte Colibri." *Tropiques* 4 (January 1942): 13–19.
———. *Two Years in the French West Indies.* New York: Harper and Brothers, 1890.
Houlberg, Marilyn. "Arts for the Water Spirits in Haitian Vodou." In *Sacred Waters: Arts for Mami Wata and Other Divinities in Africa and the Diaspora,* edited by Henry John Drewal. Bloomington: Indiana University Press, 2008.
"Idrissa Ouédraogo." imdb.com; accessed January 27, 2014.
Jonassaint, Jean. Email message to authors with comments on the draft of this book's introduction and annotations, July 25, 2012.
———. "Sur des textes fondateurs de littératures caribéennes." In *Contre-Vulgate: Essais sur nos littératures caribéennes* (forthcoming).
Kesteloot, Lilyan. "La tragédie du roi Christophe, ou les indépendances africaines au miroir d'Haïti." *Présence Africaine* 51:3 (1964): 131–45.
"Kingdom of Dahomey." *New World Encyclopedia Online*, accessed January 27, 2014.
Laville, Pierre. "Aimé Césaire et Jean-Marie Serreau: Un acte politique et poétique." *Les voies de la création théâtral* 2 (1970): 237–96.
Leconte, Vergnaud. *Henri Christophe dans l'histoire d'Haïti.* Paris: Editions Berger-Levrault, 1931.
Leiner, Jacqueline. *Aimé Césaire: Le terreau primordial.* Tübingen: Gunter Narr Verlag, 1993.
Lion Theatre @Theatre Row (announcement of 2010 New York performance of *A Season in the Congo*). http://www.theateronline.com/venuebook.xzc?PK=50425&View=Hist. Accessed January 27, 2014.
Lomax, Alan. *Recordings in Haiti 1936–1937,* with liner notes by Gage Averill, foreword by Anna Lomax Wood, and transcription of Alan Lomax's Haitian notebooks. Estate of Alan Lomax, 2009 / Harte Recordings LLS.
Manheim, Ralph. *The Tragedy of King Christophe.* Translation of acting script of *La Tragédie du roi Christophe.* New York: Grove Press, 1969.
Marx, Karl, and Friedrich Engels. *Die Heilige Familie oder Kritik der Kritischen Kritik.* Frankfurt/Vienna: Europäische Verlagsanstalt Frankfurt/Europa Verlag Wien, 1967 [1845].
Maurouard, Elvire. *Aimé Césaire et Haïti.* France: Acoria, 2009.
Mbom, Clement. *Le Théâtre d'Aimé Césaire.* France: Éditions Fernand Nathan, 1979.
Ménil, René, and Aimé Césaire. "Introduction au folklore martiniquais." *Tropiques* 4 (January 1942), 7–11.

Métraux, Alfred. *Voodoo in Haiti.* Translated by Hugo Charteris. Introduction by Sidney Mintz. New York: Schocken, 1972. (Translation of Métraux, Alfred. *Le Vaudou Haïtien.* Paris: Gallimard, 1958.)

Miller, Christopher L. *The French Atlantic Triangle: Literature and Culture of the Slave Trade.* Durham: Duke University Press, 2008.

Nesbitt, Nick. *Voicing Memory: History and Subjectivity in French Caribbean Literature.* Charlottesville and London: University of Virginia Press, 2003.

Nicholls, David. *From Dessalines to Duvalier: Race, Colour and National Independence in Haiti.* Cambridge: Cambridge University Press, 1979.

Nixon, Rob. "Caribbean and African Appropriations of *The Tempest.*" *Critical Inquiry* 13, no. 3: 557–78.

Ojo-Ade, Femi. "Problems of Translation in Black Literature: An Example of Aimé Césaire's *La tragédie du Roi Christophe.*" *Obsidian: Black Literature in Review* 4, no. 2 (Summer 1978).

Pestre de Almeida, Lilian. *Aimé Césaire: Une saison en Haiti.* Québec: Mémoire d'encrier, 2010.

Popkin, Jeremy D. *You Are All Free: The Haitian Revolution and the Abolition of Slavery.* Cambridge: Cambridge University Press, 2010.

Procès-verbal de la cérémonie du sacre et du couronnement de LL. MM. L'Empereur Napoléon et L'Impératrice Joséphine. Paris: L'Imprimerie Impériale, An XIII (1805). Available at books.google.com; accessed January 27, 2014.

Purdue University's Center for New Crops and Plant Products website, s.v. "yellow mombin." Accessed January 27, 2014. http://www.hort.pur due.edu/newcrop/morton/yellow_mombin_ars.html.

Reboux, Paul. *Blancs et noirs: Carnet de voyage: Haïti, Cuba, Jamaïque, Etats-Unis,* 139–46. Paris: Flammarion, 1919. Available at books.google .com; accessed January 27, 2014.

Régnier, Mathurin. *Oeuvres complètes.* Paris: Flammarion, n.d.

Renard, Yves. Email to Kendel Hippolyte forwarded to Paul Breslin, July 17, 2010.

Revert, Eugène. *La Martinique, étude géographique et humaine.* Paris: Nouvelles Éditions Latines, 1949. Available at books.google.com; accessed January 27, 2014.

Ruhe, Ernstpeter. *Aimé Césaire et Janheinz Jahn: Les debuts du théâtre Césairien.* Würzburg: Königshausen und Neumann, 1990.

School of Forest Resources and Conservation website, s.v. "flatwoods plum." http://www.sfrc.ufl.edu/extension/4h/ecosystems/_plants /Flatwoods_plum/index.html. Accessed January 27, 2014.

Scott, David. *Conscripts of Modernity: The Tragedy of Colonial Enlightenment.* Durham, N.C.: Duke University Press, 2004.

"Specimens of the Literature of the Negro Kingdom Established in Hayti, or St Domingo," *The Scots Magazine and Edinburgh Literary Miscellany,* vol. 78 (November 1816): 808–10; 902–9. Available at books.google.com; accessed January 27, 2014.

Targète, Jean, and Raphael G. Urciolo. *Haitian Creole-English Dictionary.* Kensington, Md: Dunwoody Press, 1993.

Thompson, Robert Farris. *Flash of the Spirit: African and Afro-American Art and Philosophy.* New York: Vintage, 1983.

Toumson, M. Roger. *Aimé Césaire: Le nègre inconsolé.* Fort-de-France, Martinique: Syros/Vents des îles, 1993.

Trouillot, Michel-Rolph. *Haiti: State against Nation: The Origins and Legacy of Duvalierism.* New York: Monthly Review Press, 1990.

———. *Silencing the Past: Power and the Production of History.* Boston: Beacon Press, 1995.

Vandercook, John W. *Black Majesty: The Life of Christophe King of Haiti.* New York: Harper & Row, 1928.

Wilberforce, Robert Isaac, and Samuel Wilberforce, eds. *The Correspondence of William Wilberforce.* 2 vols. London: J. Murray, 1840.

Youth Onstage! (announcement of 2009 New York performance of *A Season in the Congo*). http://www.enoughproject.org/events/season-congo-new-york-ny. Accessed January 27, 2014.

Zabus, Chantal. *Tempests after Shakespeare.* New York: Palgrave, 2002.